Mmmm...
Baking

Mmmm...
Baking

This edition published in 2011

LOVE FOOD is an imprint of Parragon Books Ltd

Parragon
Queen Street House
4 Queen Street
Bath BA1 1HE, UK

ISBN: 978-1-4454-2785-0

Printed in China

Design by Talking Design
Cover photography by Charlie Richards
Cover image styled by Mary Wall
Introduction by Linda Doeser

Notes for the Reader
This book uses both metric and imperial measurements. Follow the same units of
measurement throughout; do not mix metric and imperial. All spoon measurements are
level: teaspoons are assumed to be 5 ml, and tablespoons are assumed to be 15 ml.
Unless otherwise stated, milk is assumed to be full fat, eggs and individual vegetables are
medium, and pepper is freshly ground black pepper.

The times given are an approximate guide only. Preparation times differ according to the
techniques used by different people and the cooking times may also vary from those
given. Optional ingredients, variations or serving suggestions have not been included in
the calculations.

Recipes using raw or very lightly cooked eggs should be avoided by infants, the elderly,
pregnant women, convalescents and anyone suffering from an illness. Pregnant and
breastfeeding women are advised to avoid eating peanuts and peanut products.
Sufferers from nut allergies should be aware that some of the ready-made ingredients
used in the recipes in this book may contain nuts. Always check the packaging before use.

contents

introduction

The aroma of warm bread straight from the oven or a freshly baked cake must be one of the most appetizing and evocative smells in the world. Home-made muffins, cupcakes and biscuits make the perfect any-time snack, while a luxurious layered gateau is the crowning glory of any celebration meal. Whether a batch of scones that can be whipped up in moments by even an inexperienced cook or a melt-in-the-mouth pastry that needs a light touch and rather more time, there is something very special about home-baked treats.

Baking is one of the most satisfying kinds of cooking, but for some reason it has a reputation for being time-consuming and complicated. This couldn't be further from the truth – muffins, cupcakes, brownies, bars and biscuits take very little time and, providing you follow a few basic rules, the results will always be far more appealing and much tastier than anything you can buy. New twists on family favourites combine innovation and tradition, while anyone with a creative urge can really push the boat out with fabulous iced, layered and chocolate-topped confections that look almost too lovely to eat. If you're feeling a little fed up, why not work off your frustrations by kneading bread dough and then bask in a warm glow of self-satisfaction as you cut the first delicious slice of the loaf? Of course, not everyone has a sweet tooth and anyway there are many occasions when savouries are the order of the day. There's something so much more rewarding about serving home-made quiches, tartlets and crackers instead of the more usual peanuts and crisps. However, be warned that your home-baked delicacies, sweet or savoury, are not likely to hang around for very long and you will soon become the most popular host in the neighbourhood.

top tips for success

- Keep an eye on 'use-by' dates. If kept too long, flour and nuts will go rancid, dried fruit will become mouldy, spices will lose their aroma and flavour, and yeast will die.

- Precise measurement of ingredients is more important with baking than with any other kind of cooking and makes the difference between success and failure. If the proportions of fat, flour and egg, for example, are incorrect, a cake will be heavy and doughy.

- Don't substitute ingredients. Different flours vary in their characteristics, particularly in the quantity of liquid they will absorb. As a general rule, plain flour is used for pastry doughs; self-raising flour, which includes added baking powder, for cakes and scones; and strong flour, with its high gluten content, for bread. The most commonly used fat is butter, not least because it has the richest flavour. Firm margarine, sold in blocks, lacks the flavour of butter but may be used in the same way. Soft margarine, sold in tubs, is specified in some recipes. However, do not use low-fat spreads as these simply do not work with most cakes and pastries.

- With the exception of pastry doughs, which should be kept as cool as possible, all forms of baking work better if all the ingredients have been brought to room temperature before you start. Remove eggs and fat from the refrigerator about 30 minutes in advance.

- Pastry doughs should be handled as little as possible and kept cool. Put the mixing bowl and a jug of water into the refrigerator to chill 30 minutes beforehand. Rinse your hands in cold water (and dry thoroughly) before rubbing fat into flour or use a pastry blender. Grating the fat into the flour reduces the amount of time required for rubbing in and is a good trick on a hot day. A marble slab and rolling pin are ideal for rolling out the dough as they help keep it cool.

- Pastry doughs should always be rested in the refrigerator before rolling out. This enables the gluten, a protein in the flour that starts to react when the liquid is added, to become firm and elastic. This makes the dough easy to roll out and helps to prevent it from shrinking during cooking.

- Many people are hesitant about using yeast and so don't make bread, but these days you can't go wrong with easy-blend dried yeast. This concentrated dried yeast is added with the dry ingredients – flour and salt, for example – and there is no need to mix it with water first. Fresh and ordinary dried yeast must be activated before they are used.

- Always use the size and shape tin specified in the recipe, especially when making cakes. If the tin is too large, the cake will be flat; if it is too small, the centre will bulge or the mixture will run over the sides. Some recipes give the tin's capacity – to find this simply use a measuring jug to pour water into the tin and note how much water it takes to fill it.

- Preheat the oven to the required temperature and avoid opening the oven door during baking, especially with cakes as the sudden draught of colder air will make them collapse. Use a timer to estimate when the cake is likely to be cooked and test by inserting a fine skewer into the centre. If it comes out clean, the cake is ready. Test sponge cakes by pressing the top lightly with your finger; it should spring back immediately and the cake should have shrunk slightly from the sides of the tin.

- Follow the recipe instructions for cooling. Light cakes are turned out onto a wire rack 3–5 minutes after they come out of the oven and while they are still warm, but heavy cakes are best left to cool in the tin. Some delicate biscuits should be left on the baking trays to firm up before being transferred to a wire rack. Always use a wire rack to allow air to circulate to prevent cakes, biscuits and loaves from becoming soggy.

shortcrust pastry

makes 225 g/8 oz
- 225 g/8 oz plain flour
- 115 g/4 oz butter, chilled
- 2–3 tbsp cold water

1 Sift the flour into a bowl. Cut the butter into small cubes and add to the flour. Rub in using your fingertips, lifting your hands high above the bowl to incorporate more air. The mixture will resemble fine breadcrumbs when the butter has been fully rubbed in. Gradually add the water and use your fingers to bring the dough together.

2 Alternatively, use a food processor to make the pastry. Put the flour and butter in the processor and process until the mixture resembles fine breadcrumbs. At this stage, you can either add the water to the machine and process until the pastry comes together, or tip the flour and butter mixture into a bowl and add the water by hand.

3 Turn out the dough onto a lightly floured work surface and knead very lightly. The pastry should be wrapped in clingfilm and chilled in the refrigerator for 30 minutes before rolling.

puff pastry

makes 350 g/12 oz
- 350 g/12 oz plain flour
- 175 g/6 oz butter
- 8 tbsp cold water

1 Sift the flour into a bowl and rub in 40 g/1½ oz of the butter. Add the water and use your fingers to bring the mixture together. Knead briefly to form a smooth dough. Put in a polythene bag and chill for 30 minutes.

2 Roll out the remaining butter between 2 sheets of clingfilm to form a block about 1 cm/½ inch thick. Roll out the dough to a square about 4 times the size of the block of butter. Put the block of butter in the centre of the dough and fold over the corners of the dough to completely enclose the butter. Roll out the dough into a rectangle 3 times as long as it is wide. Fold a third of the dough over to cover the middle third, then fold the remainder over the top. Give the dough a half turn, roll out to form another rectangle and fold again as before. Repeat the initial rolling and folding 6 times in total, chilling the dough between rolling.

3 Leave to chill for a final 30 minutes, then use as required.

Mmmm...
cakes

chocolate slab cake

serves 9
- 200 g/7 oz unsalted butter, plus extra for greasing
- 100 g/3½ oz plain chocolate, broken into pieces
- 75 ml/2½ fl oz water
- 350 g/12 oz plain flour
- 2 tsp baking powder
- 250 g/9 oz soft light brown sugar
- 75 ml/2½ fl oz soured cream
- 2 eggs, beaten

icing
- 200 g/7 oz plain chocolate, broken into pieces
- 6 tbsp water
- 3 tbsp single cream
- 15 g/½ oz unsalted butter, chilled

1 Preheat the oven to 190°C/375°F/Gas Mark 5. Grease and base-line a 23-cm/9-inch square cake tin.

2 Melt the butter and chocolate with the water in a saucepan over a low heat, stirring frequently. Sift the flour and baking powder into a mixing bowl and stir in the sugar. Pour in the chocolate mixture and beat well until all of the ingredients are evenly mixed. Stir in the soured cream, followed by the eggs.

3 Pour the mixture into the prepared cake tin. Bake in the preheated oven for 40–45 minutes, until springy to the touch.

4 Leave the cake to cool slightly in the tin before turning it out onto a wire rack. Leave to cool completely.

5 To make the icing, melt the chocolate with the water in a saucepan over a very low heat, stir in the cream and remove from the heat. Stir in the butter, then pour the icing over the cooled cake, using a palette knife to spread it evenly over the top. Leave to set before slicing.

chocolate & orange semolina cake

serves 8

- 1 large orange
- 100 g/3½ oz caster sugar
- 2 eggs
- 85 g/3 oz unsalted butter, melted, plus extra for greasing
- 175 g/6 oz semolina
- 55 g/2 oz cocoa powder
- 1½ tsp baking powder
- icing sugar, for dusting

1 Preheat the oven to 180°C/350°F/Gas Mark 4. Grease and base-line a 20-cm/8-inch round cake tin.

2 Coarsely grate the rind from the orange and reserve. With a sharp knife, cut away all the remaining peel and white pith, then cut the flesh into small pieces, reserving the juices.

3 Place the sugar and eggs in a bowl and whisk vigorously with an electric mixer until pale and foamy. Whisk in the melted butter gradually, pouring a thin steady stream as you whisk. Sift over the semolina, cocoa powder and baking powder, and fold in lightly and evenly. Stir in the orange pieces with their juices and mix to a soft batter.

4 Spoon the mixture into the prepared tin, smoothing level with a palette knife. Bake in the preheated oven for 35–40 minutes, until just firm to the touch. Leave to cool in the tin for 5 minutes, then turn out onto a wire rack to cool completely.

5 To decorate, scatter with the reserved grated orange rind and dust with icing sugar.

marbled chocolate & vanilla ring

serves 12

- oil or melted butter, for greasing
- 175 g/6 oz plain flour
- 1 tbsp baking powder
- 175 g/6 oz unsalted butter, softened
- 175 g/6 oz caster sugar
- 3 eggs, beaten
- 2 tbsp cocoa powder
- 2 tbsp milk
- 1 tsp vanilla extract
- icing sugar, for dusting

1 Preheat the oven to 160°C/325°F/Gas Mark 3. Grease a 1.5-litre/2¾-pint ring cake tin, preferably non-stick.

2 Sift the flour and baking powder into a large bowl and add the butter, caster sugar and eggs. Beat well until the mixture is smooth. Transfer half the mixture to a separate bowl.

3 Mix the cocoa powder with the milk and stir into 1 bowl of mixture. Add the vanilla extract to the other bowl and mix evenly. Spoon alternate tablespoons of the 2 mixtures into the prepared tin and swirl lightly with a palette knife for a marbled effect.

4 Bake in the preheated oven for 40–50 minutes, or until risen, firm and golden brown. Leave to cool in the tin for 10 minutes, then turn out and finish cooling on a wire rack. Dust with icing sugar before serving.

victoria sponge cake

serves 8–10

- 175 g/6 oz unsalted butter, softened, plus extra for greasing
- 175 g/6 oz caster sugar
- 3 eggs, beaten
- 175 g/6 oz self-raising flour
- pinch of salt
- 3 tbsp raspberry jam
- 1 tbsp icing sugar

1 Preheat the oven to 180°C/350°F/Gas Mark 4. Grease and base-line 2 x 20-cm/8-inch sandwich cake tins.

2 Cream the butter and caster sugar together in a mixing bowl using a wooden spoon or an electric mixer until the mixture is pale in colour and light and fluffy. Add the eggs a little at a time, beating well after each addition. Sift the flour and salt into a separate bowl and carefully add to the mixture, folding in with a metal spoon or a spatula.

3 Divide the mixture between the prepared tins and smooth over with the spatula. Place them on the same shelf in the centre of the oven and bake for 25–30 minutes, until well risen, golden brown and beginning to shrink from the sides of the tin.

4 Leave to cool in the tins for 1 minute, then turn out onto a wire rack to cool. When completely cool, sandwich together the cakes with the jam and dust with the icing sugar.

jewel-topped madeira cake

serves 8-10

- 225 g/8 oz unsalted butter, softened, plus extra for greasing
- 225 g/8 oz golden caster sugar
- finely grated rind of 1 lemon
- 4 eggs, beaten
- 350 g/12 oz self-raising flour, sifted
- 2–3 tbsp milk

fruit topping

- 2½ tbsp honey
- 300 g/10½ oz glacé fruit, sliced

1 Preheat the oven to 160°C/325°F/Gas Mark 3. Grease and line a 20-cm/8-inch round cake tin.

2 Put the butter, sugar and lemon rind in a bowl and beat together until light and fluffy. Gradually beat in the eggs. Gently fold in the flour, adding enough of the milk to give a soft dropping consistency.

3 Spoon the mixture into the prepared tin. Bake in the preheated oven for 1½–1¾ hours, until risen and golden and a skewer inserted into the centre comes out clean.

4 Leave to cool in the tin for 10 minutes, then turn out onto a wire rack to cool. For the topping, brush the honey over the top of the cake and arrange the glacé fruit on top.

honey & almond cake

serves 8

- 75 g/2¾ oz soft margarine, plus extra for greasing
- 75 g/2¾ oz soft light brown sugar
- 2 eggs
- 175 g/6 oz self-raising flour
- 1 tsp baking powder
- 4 tbsp milk
- 2 tbsp honey
- 50 g/1¾ oz flaked almonds

syrup

- 225 g/8 oz honey
- 2 tbsp lemon juice

1 Preheat the oven to 180°C/350°F/Gas Mark 4. Grease and line an 18-cm/7-inch round cake tin.

2 Place the margarine, sugar, eggs, flour, baking powder, milk and honey in a large mixing bowl and beat well with a wooden spoon for about 1 minute, or until all of the ingredients are thoroughly mixed together.

3 Spoon into the prepared tin, smooth the surface with the back of a spoon or a knife and sprinkle with the flaked almonds.

4 Bake in the preheated oven for about 50 minutes, or until well risen and a skewer inserted into the centre comes out clean.

5 Meanwhile, make the syrup. Combine the honey and lemon juice in a small saucepan and simmer over a low heat for about 5 minutes, or until the syrup coats the back of a spoon.

6 As soon as the cake comes out of the oven, pour the syrup over it, allowing it to soak into the cake. Leave the cake to cool in the tin for at least 2 hours before slicing.

coconut & lime cake

serves 8

- 175 g/6 oz unsalted butter, softened, plus extra for greasing
- 175 g/6 oz caster sugar
- 3 eggs, beaten
- 150 g/5½ oz self-raising flour
- 85 g/3 oz desiccated coconut
- grated rind and juice of 1 lime
- 25 g/1 oz shredded coconut, lightly toasted

icing

- 175 g/6 oz icing sugar
- grated rind and juice of 1 lime

1 Preheat the oven to 160°C/325°F/Gas Mark 3. Grease and line a 20-cm/8-inch round cake tin.

2 Place the butter and caster sugar in a large bowl and beat together until pale and fluffy. Gradually beat in the eggs. Sift in the flour and gently fold in using a metal spoon. Fold in the desiccated coconut, lime rind and juice.

3 Spoon the mixture into the prepared tin and level the surface. Bake in the preheated oven for 1–1¼ hours, until risen, golden and firm to the touch. Leave to cool in the tin for 5 minutes, then turn out onto a wire rack to cool completely.

4 For the icing, sift the icing sugar into a bowl. Stir in the lime rind and juice to make a thick, smooth icing, adding a few drops of water, if necessary. Spoon the icing over the top of the cake, allowing it to drizzle down the sides of the cake. Scatter the toasted shredded coconut over the icing and leave to set.

coffee streusel cake

serves 8–10

- 225 g/8 oz plain flour
- 1 tbsp baking powder
- 70 g/2½ oz caster sugar
- 150 ml/5 fl oz milk
- 2 eggs
- 115 g/4 oz unsalted butter, melted and cooled, plus extra for greasing
- 2 tbsp instant coffee granules, dissolved in 1 tbsp boiling water
- 50 g/1¾ oz chopped almonds
- icing sugar, for dusting

topping

- 70 g/2½ oz self-raising flour
- 70 g/2½ oz demerara sugar
- 25 g/1 oz unsalted butter, cut into small pieces
- 1 tsp ground mixed spice
- 1 tbsp water

1 Preheat the oven to 190°C/375°F/Gas Mark 5. Grease and line a 23-cm/9-inch loose-based round cake tin.

2 Sift the plain flour and baking powder into a mixing bowl, then stir in the caster sugar.

3 Whisk the milk, eggs, melted butter and coffee mixture together and pour onto the dry ingredients. Add the almonds and mix lightly together. Spoon the mixture into the prepared tin.

4 To make the topping, mix the self-raising flour and demerara sugar together in a bowl. Rub in the butter with your fingertips until the mixture resembles breadcrumbs. Sprinkle in the mixed spice and water and bring the mixture together in loose crumbs. Sprinkle the topping evenly over the cake.

5 Bake in the preheated oven for 50 minutes–1 hour. Cover loosely with foil if the topping starts to brown too quickly.

6 Leave to cool in the tin. Remove the cake from the tin and dust with icing sugar just before serving.

glazed fruit & nut cake

serves 16–18

- oil or melted butter, for greasing
- 250 g/9 oz plain flour, plus extra for sprinkling
- 1 tbsp baking powder
- 1 tsp ground mixed spice
- 175 g/6 oz unsalted butter, softened
- 175 g/6 oz dark muscovado sugar
- 3 eggs, beaten
- 1 tsp vanilla extract
- 2 tbsp milk
- 300 g/10½ oz mixed dried fruit
- 85 g/3 oz chopped mixed nuts

to decorate

- 3 tbsp honey, warmed
- 350 g/12 oz mixed glacé fruits, such as pineapple, cherries and orange
- 55 g/2 oz whole shelled nuts, such as Brazil nuts, almonds and walnuts

1 Preheat the oven to 160°C/325°F/Gas Mark 3. Grease a 23-cm/9-inch round springform cake tin and sprinkle with a little flour to coat, shaking out the excess.

2 Sift the flour, baking powder and mixed spice into a large bowl and add the butter, sugar, eggs and vanilla extract. Beat well until the mixture is smooth, then stir in the milk, mixed dried fruit and chopped mixed nuts.

3 Spoon the mixture into the prepared tin and smooth the surface with a palette knife. Bake in the preheated oven for about 1 hour, or until risen, firm and golden brown.

4 Leave to cool in the tin for 30 minutes, then remove the sides and place on a wire rack to finish cooling.

5 Brush the top of the cake with a little of the warmed honey, then arrange the glacé fruits and whole shelled nuts on top. Brush with the remaining honey and leave to set.

date & spice loaf

serves 8–10

- oil or melted butter, for greasing
- 85 g/3 oz white plain flour
- 100 g/3½ oz wholemeal plain flour
- 1 tbsp baking powder
- 1 tsp ground mixed spice
- 175 g/6 oz unsalted butter, softened
- 175 g/6 oz golden caster sugar
- 3 eggs, beaten
- 1 tsp vanilla extract
- 175 g/6 oz stoned dates, roughly chopped

1 Preheat the oven to 160°C/325°F/Gas Mark 3. Grease and line a 1.3-litre/2¼-pint loaf tin.

2 Sift the flours, baking powder and mixed spice into a large bowl, adding any bran left in the sieve. Add the butter, sugar, eggs and vanilla extract. Beat well until the mixture is smooth, then stir in half the dates.

3 Spoon the mixture into the prepared tin and scatter over the remaining dates. Bake in the preheated oven for 40–50 minutes, or until risen, firm and golden brown.

4 Leave to cool in the tin for 10 minutes, then turn out and finish cooling on a wire rack.

gingerbread with lemon drizzle

serves 9
- butter, for greasing
- 175 g/6 oz self-raising flour
- 1 tbsp ground ginger
- 2 eggs
- 100 g/3½ oz light muscovado sugar
- 4 tbsp black treacle
- 4 tbsp milk
- 4 tbsp sunflower oil

to decorate
- 100 g/3½ oz icing sugar
- ½ tsp lemon extract
- 1 tbsp edible silver balls

1 Preheat the oven to 180°C/350°F/Gas Mark 4. Grease and base-line a 19-cm/7½-inch square cake tin.

2 Sift the flour and ginger together into a bowl. In a separate bowl, beat together the eggs, muscovado sugar, treacle, milk and oil. Make a well in the dry ingredients and add the liquid mixture, beating thoroughly until the mixture is smooth.

3 Pour the mixture into the prepared tin. Bake in the preheated oven for 25–30 minutes, or until risen and springy to the touch. Leave to cool in the tin for 5 minutes, then turn out and finish cooling on a wire rack.

4 Mix the icing sugar with the lemon extract and enough water to make a fairly thick paste. Drizzle over the cake and sprinkle with the silver balls. Cut into squares when set.

frosting-topped carrot cake

serves 12
- butter, for greasing
- 2 eggs
- 175 g/6 oz light muscovado sugar
- 200 ml/7 fl oz sunflower oil
- 200 g/7 oz carrot, coarsely grated
- 225 g/8 oz wholemeal plain flour
- 1 tsp bicarbonate of soda
- 2 tsp ground cinnamon
- 1 tsp ground nutmeg
- 115 g/4 oz walnuts, roughly chopped

frosting
- 115 g/4 oz half-fat cream cheese
- 50 g/1¾ oz unsalted butter, softened
- 85 g/3 oz icing sugar
- 1 tsp grated lemon rind
- 1 tsp grated orange rind

1 Preheat the oven to 190°C/375°F/Gas Mark 5. Grease and line a 23-cm/9-inch square cake tin.

2 In a mixing bowl, beat the eggs until well blended, then add the muscovado sugar and oil. Mix well and add the grated carrot. Sift in the flour, bicarbonate of soda and spices, then add the walnuts. Mix together until well incorporated.

3 Spoon the mixture into the prepared tin and smooth the surface with a palette knife. Bake in the preheated oven for 40–50 minutes, until the cake is risen, firm to the touch and has begun to shrink away slightly from the edges of the tin. Leave to cool in the tin until just warm, then turn out onto a wire rack.

4 To make the frosting, put all the ingredients into a mixing bowl and beat together for 2–3 minutes, until smooth. When the cake is completely cold, spread with the frosting, smooth over with a fork and leave to firm up a little before slicing.

walnut & banana cake

serves 12

- 250 g/9 oz wholemeal plain flour
- 1 tsp salt
- 1 heaped tsp baking powder
- 1 tsp ground cinnamon
- 4 ripe bananas
- 100 ml/3½ fl oz groundnut oil, plus extra for oiling
- 25 g/1 oz unsalted butter, softened
- 175 g/6 oz soft light brown sugar
- 2 large eggs, beaten
- 175 g/6 oz walnut pieces

1 Preheat the oven to 180°C/350°F/Gas Mark 4. Lightly oil a 1-kg/2 lb 4-oz loaf tin.

2 Sift the flour, salt, baking powder and cinnamon into a large bowl, adding any bran left in the sieve. Stir thoroughly with a fork.

3 Peel the bananas and mash with a fork. Add to the bowl with all the remaining ingredients, except the walnuts. Using an electric mixer, beat the mixture until smooth. Alternatively, use a wooden spoon. Fold in the walnuts.

4 Spoon the mixture into the prepared tin and level the surface. Bake in the preheated oven for 1–1¼ hours, or until a skewer inserted into the centre comes out clean. Leave to cool in the tin for 5 minutes, then turn out onto a wire rack to cool completely before serving.

cherry & almond cake

serves 8

- 300 g/10½ oz glacé cherries
- 175 g/6 oz unsalted butter, softened, plus extra for greasing
- 175 g/6 oz golden caster sugar
- 3 eggs
- 40 g/1½ oz ground almonds
- 280 g/10 oz plain flour
- 1½ tsp baking powder
- 70 g/2½ oz flaked almonds

1 Preheat the oven to 160°C/325°F/Gas Mark 3. Grease and line an 18-cm/7-inch square cake tin.

2 Cut the cherries in half, then put them in a sieve and rinse to remove all the syrup. Pat dry with kitchen paper and set aside.

3 Put the butter, sugar, eggs and ground almonds in a bowl. Sift in the flour and baking powder. Beat thoroughly until smooth, then stir in the cherries. Spoon the mixture into the prepared tin and smooth the top. Sprinkle the flaked almonds over the cake mixture.

4 Bake in the preheated oven for 1½–1¾ hours, until well risen and a skewer inserted into the centre of the cake comes out clean.

5 Leave in the tin for 10 minutes, then turn out onto a wire rack to cool.

pear & ginger cake

serves 8–10

- 200 g/7 oz unsalted butter, softened, plus extra for greasing
- 200 g/7 oz caster sugar
- 200 g/7 oz self-raising flour
- 1 tbsp ground ginger
- 3 eggs, lightly beaten
- 450 g/1 lb pears, peeled, cored and thinly sliced
- 1 tbsp soft light brown sugar

1 Preheat the oven to 180°C/350°F/Gas Mark 4. Grease and line a 20-cm/8-inch round cake tin.

2 Put 175 g/6 oz of the butter and the caster sugar into a bowl. Sift in the flour and ground ginger and add the eggs. Beat well with a whisk until smooth.

3 Spoon the mixture into the prepared tin, smoothing the surface with a palette knife. Arrange the pear slices over the cake mixture. Sprinkle with the brown sugar and dot with the remaining butter.

4 Bake in the preheated oven for 35–40 minutes, or until the cake is golden and feels springy to the touch.

5 Leave the cake to cool slightly in the tin, then turn out onto a wire rack to cool completely.

spiced apple & sultana cake

serves 8–10

- 225 g/8 oz unsalted butter, softened, plus extra for greasing
- 225 g/8 oz light muscovado sugar
- 4 large eggs, lightly beaten
- 225 g/8 oz self-raising flour
- 2 tsp ground cinnamon
- ½ tsp ground nutmeg
- 85 g/3 oz sultanas
- 3 small apples, peeled, cored and thinly sliced
- 2 tbsp honey, warmed

1 Preheat the oven to 180°C/350°F/Gas Mark 4. Grease and line a 23-cm/9-inch round springform cake tin.

2 Place the butter and sugar in a large bowl and beat together until light and fluffy. Gradually beat in the eggs. Sift the flour, cinnamon and nutmeg into the mixture and fold in gently using a metal spoon. Fold in the sultanas.

3 Spoon half the mixture into the prepared tin and level the surface. Scatter over half the sliced apples. Spoon over the remaining cake mixture and gently level the surface. Arrange the remaining apple slices over the top.

4 Bake in the preheated oven for 1–1¼ hours, until risen, golden brown and firm to the touch. Leave to cool in the tin for 10 minutes, then turn out onto a wire rack. Brush the top with the warmed honey and leave to cool completely.

blueberry orange streusel cake

serves 8-10

- oil or melted butter, for greasing
- 175 g/6 oz plain flour
- 2 tsp baking powder
- 175 g/6 oz unsalted butter, softened
- 175 g/6 oz caster sugar
- 3 eggs, beaten
- 1 tsp vanilla extract
- finely grated rind of ½ orange
- 55 g/2 oz ground almonds
- 125 g/4½ oz fresh blueberries

topping

- 55 g/2 oz plain flour
- 25 g/1 oz unsalted butter, softened
- 25 g/1 oz caster sugar
- finely grated rind of ½ orange

1 Preheat the oven to 160°C/325°F/Gas Mark 3. Grease and base-line a 23-cm/9-inch round springform cake tin.

2 For the topping, place all the ingredients in a bowl and stir with a fork to make a crumbly mixture.

3 Sift the flour and baking powder into a large bowl and add the butter, sugar, eggs and vanilla extract. Beat well until the mixture is smooth, then add the orange rind, ground almonds and half the blueberries.

4 Spoon the mixture into the prepared tin, smooth the surface with a palette knife and scatter over the remaining blueberries. Sprinkle over the topping, covering completely.

5 Bake in the preheated oven for 1 hour–1 hour 10 minutes, or until risen, firm and golden brown. Leave to cool in the tin for 10 minutes, then remove the sides of the tin and finish cooling on a wire rack.

lemon drizzle loaf

serves 8-10
- oil or melted butter, for greasing
- 175 g/6 oz plain flour
- 1 tbsp baking powder
- 175 g/6 oz unsalted butter, softened
- 175 g/6 oz golden caster sugar
- 3 eggs, beaten
- 1 egg yolk
- finely grated rind of 1 lemon
- 2 tbsp lemon juice
- fine strips of lemon zest, to decorate

syrup
- 85 g/3 oz icing sugar
- 3 tbsp lemon juice

1 Preheat the oven to 180°C/350°F/Gas Mark 4. Grease and line a 1.2-litre/2-pint loaf tin.

2 Sift the flour and baking powder into a large bowl and add the butter, caster sugar, eggs and egg yolk. Beat well until the mixture is smooth, then stir in the lemon rind and juice.

3 Spoon the mixture into the prepared tin and smooth the surface with a palette knife. Bake in the preheated oven for 40–50 minutes, or until well risen, firm and golden brown.

4 Remove the tin from the oven and transfer to a wire rack. For the syrup, place the icing sugar and lemon juice in a saucepan and heat gently without boiling, stirring until the sugar dissolves.

5 Prick the top of the loaf several times with a skewer and spoon over the syrup. Leave to cool completely in the tin, then turn out, scatter with strips of lemon zest and cut into slices.

clementine cake

serves 8

- 175 g/6 oz unsalted butter, softened, plus extra for greasing
- 175 g/6 oz caster sugar
- grated rind of 2 clementines
- 3 eggs, beaten
- 175 g/6 oz self-raising flour
- 3 tbsp ground almonds
- 3 tbsp single cream

glaze & topping

- 6 tbsp clementine juice
- 2 tbsp caster sugar
- 3 white sugar cubes, crushed

1 Preheat the oven to 180°C/350°F/Gas Mark 4. Grease and base-line an 18-cm/7-inch round cake tin.

2 In a bowl, cream together the butter, caster sugar and clementine rind until pale and fluffy. Gradually add the beaten eggs to the mixture, beating thoroughly after each addition.

3 Gently fold in the flour, followed by the ground almonds and cream. Spoon the mixture into the prepared tin.

4 Bake in the preheated oven for 55–60 minutes, or until a skewer inserted into the centre comes out clean. Leave to cool slightly in the tin.

5 Meanwhile, make the glaze. Put the clementine juice into a small saucepan with the caster sugar. Bring to the boil and simmer for 5 minutes.

6 Transfer the cake to a wire rack. Drizzle the glaze over the cake until it has been absorbed and sprinkle with the crushed sugar cubes.

butternut squash & orange cake

serves 6–8

- 175 g/6 oz unsalted butter, softened, plus extra for greasing
- 175 g/6 oz soft light brown sugar
- 3 eggs, beaten
- finely grated rind of 1 orange
- 225 g/8 oz wholemeal self-raising flour
- 1 tsp baking powder
- 1 tsp ground cinnamon
- 225 g/8 oz prepared butternut squash flesh (peeled and seeded weight), coarsely grated
- 115 g/4 oz sultanas
- juice of 1 orange
- 225 g/8 oz full-fat soft cheese
- 55 g/2 oz icing sugar, sifted
- strips of orange zest, to decorate

1 Preheat the oven to 180°C/350°F/Gas Mark 4. Grease and line an 18-cm/7-inch round cake tin.

2 Cream the butter and brown sugar together in a bowl until light and fluffy. Gradually beat in the eggs, beating well after each addition. Reserve 1 teaspoon of the orange rind for the topping, then beat the remaining orange rind into the creamed mixture. Fold in the flour, baking powder and cinnamon, then stir in the squash, sultanas and about 1 tablespoon of the orange juice, if necessary, to give a fairly soft consistency. Spoon the mixture into the prepared tin and level the surface.

3 Bake in the preheated oven for about 1 hour, or until risen, firm to the touch and golden brown. Remove from the oven and leave to cool in the tin for a few minutes, then turn out onto a wire rack to cool completely.

4 To make the topping, beat together the soft cheese, icing sugar, reserved grated orange rind and 2–3 teaspoons of the remaining orange juice in a bowl until smooth and combined. Spread over the top of the cold cake, swirling it attractively, then decorate with strips of orange zest.

Mmmm...
small cakes & slices

vanilla-frosted cupcakes

makes 12
- 115 g/4 oz butter, softened
- 115 g/4 oz caster sugar
- 2 eggs, lightly beaten
- 115 g/4 oz self-raising flour
- 1 tbsp milk
- 1 tbsp hundreds and thousands

frosting
- 175 g/6 oz unsalted butter, softened
- 1 tsp vanilla extract
- 280 g/10 oz icing sugar

1 Preheat the oven to 180°C/350°F/Gas Mark 4. Put 12 paper cupcake cases in a bun tin, or put 12 double-layer paper cases on a baking tray.

2 Put the butter and caster sugar in a bowl and beat together until light and fluffy. Gradually beat in the eggs. Sift in the flour and, using a metal spoon, fold into the mixture with the milk. Spoon the mixture into the paper cases.

3 Bake the cupcakes in the preheated oven for 20 minutes, or until golden brown and firm to the touch. Transfer to a wire rack and leave to cool.

4 To make the frosting, put the butter and vanilla extract in a bowl and, using an electric mixer, beat until the butter is pale and very soft. Gradually sift in the icing sugar, whisking well after each addition.

5 When the cupcakes are cold, spoon the frosting into a large piping bag fitted with a medium star-shaped nozzle and pipe a large swirl of frosting on the top of each cupcake. Sprinkle with the hundreds and thousands.

lemon butterfly cupcakes

makes 12
- 115 g/4 oz self-raising flour
- ½ tsp baking powder
- 115 g/4 oz soft margarine
- 115 g/4 oz caster sugar
- 2 eggs, lightly beaten
- finely grated rind of
  ½ lemon
- 2 tbsp milk

lemon filling
- 85 g/3 oz unsalted butter,
  softened
- 175 g/6 oz icing sugar
- 1 tbsp lemon juice

1 Preheat the oven to 190°C/375°F/Gas Mark 5. Put 12 paper cupcake cases in a bun tin, or put 12 double-layer paper cases on a baking tray.

2 Sift the flour and baking powder into a large bowl. Add the margarine, caster sugar, eggs, lemon rind and milk and, using an electric mixer, beat together until smooth. Spoon the mixture into the paper cases.

3 Bake in the preheated oven for 15–20 minutes, or until well risen and golden brown. Transfer to a wire rack and leave to cool.

4 To make the filling, put the butter in a bowl and beat until fluffy. Sift in the icing sugar, add the lemon juice and beat together until smooth and creamy.

5 When the cupcakes are cold, use a serrated knife to cut a circle from the top of each cupcake and then cut each circle in half. Spread or pipe a little of the filling on top of each cupcake, then press the 2 semi-circles of cake into it at an angle to resemble butterfly wings.

double ginger cupcakes

makes 12
- 175 g/6 oz plain flour
- 1 tbsp baking powder
- 2 tsp ground ginger
- 175 g/6 oz unsalted butter, softened
- 175 g/6 oz light muscovado sugar
- 3 eggs, beaten
- 25 g/1 oz crystallized stem ginger, finely chopped, plus extra to decorate

frosting
- 200 g/7 oz ricotta cheese
- 85 g/3 oz icing sugar, sifted
- finely grated rind of 1 tangerine

1 Preheat the oven to 190°C/375°F/Gas Mark 5. Put 12 paper cupcake cases in a bun tin, or put 12 double-layer paper cases on a baking tray.

2 Sift the flour, baking powder and ground ginger into a large bowl. Add the butter, muscovado sugar and eggs and beat well until smooth. Stir in the crystallized ginger. Spoon the mixture into the paper cases.

3 Bake in the preheated oven for 15–20 minutes, until well risen. Transfer to a wire rack and leave to cool.

4 For the frosting, mix together the ricotta, icing sugar and tangerine rind until smooth.

5 Spoon a little frosting onto each cupcake and spread over the surface to cover. Decorate with crystallized ginger.

chocolate hazelnut cupcakes

makes 18

- 175 g/6 oz unsalted butter, softened
- 115 g/4 oz soft light brown sugar
- 2 large eggs, lightly beaten
- 2 tbsp chocolate hazelnut spread
- 175 g/6 oz self-raising flour
- 50 g/1¾ oz blanched hazelnuts, roughly ground

topping

- 5 tbsp chocolate hazelnut spread
- 18 whole blanched hazelnuts

1 Preheat the oven to 180°C/350°F/Gas Mark 4. Put 18 paper cupcake cases in 2 bun tins or put 18 double-layer paper cases on a large baking tray.

2 Put the butter and sugar in a mixing bowl and beat together until light and fluffy. Gradually beat in the eggs, then stir in the chocolate hazelnut spread. Sift in the flour and, using a metal spoon, fold into the mixture with the ground hazelnuts. Spoon the mixture into the paper cases.

3 Bake in the preheated oven for 20–25 minutes, or until risen and firm to the touch. Transfer to a wire rack and leave to cool.

4 When the cupcakes are cold, swirl some chocolate hazelnut spread over the top of each cupcake and top with a hazelnut.

jam doughnut muffins

makes 12

- oil or melted butter, for greasing
- 280 g/10 oz plain flour
- 1 tbsp baking powder
- ⅛ tsp salt
- 115 g/4 oz caster sugar
- 2 eggs
- 200 ml/7 fl oz milk
- 6 tbsp sunflower oil or 85 g/ 3 oz unsalted butter, melted and cooled
- 1 tsp vanilla extract
- 12 tsp raspberry or strawberry jam

topping

- 115 g/4 oz butter
- 150 g/5½ oz granulated sugar

1 Preheat the oven to 200°C/400°F/Gas Mark 6. Grease the holes in a 12-cup muffin tin.

2 Sift together the flour, baking powder and salt into a large bowl. Stir in the caster sugar.

3 Lightly beat the eggs in a large jug or bowl, then beat in the milk, oil and vanilla extract. Make a well in the centre of the dry ingredients and pour in the beaten liquid ingredients. Stir gently until just combined; do not over-mix.

4 Spoon half of the mixture into the prepared muffin tin. Add a teaspoon of jam to the centre of each, then spoon in the remaining mixture. Bake in the preheated oven for about 20 minutes, until well risen, golden brown and firm to the touch.

5 Meanwhile, prepare the topping. Melt the butter. Spread the granulated sugar in a wide, shallow bowl. When the muffins are baked, leave in the tin for 5 minutes. Dip the tops of the muffins in the melted butter, then roll in the sugar. Serve warm or transfer to a wire rack and leave to cool.

blueberry bran muffins

makes 10

- 150 g/5½ oz white plain flour
- 100 g/3½ oz light brown self-raising flour
- 1 tbsp oat bran
- 2 tsp baking powder
- ½ tsp bicarbonate of soda
- pinch of salt
- 50 g/1¾ oz demerara sugar
- 1 tbsp honey
- 1 large egg
- 200 ml/7 fl oz buttermilk
- 150 g/5½ oz fresh blueberries

1 Preheat the oven to 180°C/350°F/Gas Mark 4. Put 10 paper muffin cases in a muffin tin, or put 10 double-layer paper cases on a baking tray.

2 Mix together the flours, bran, baking powder, bicarbonate of soda and salt in a bowl and stir in the sugar. Whisk the honey, egg and buttermilk together in a jug.

3 Pour the wet ingredients into the dry and stir gently until just combined; do not over-mix. Fold in the blueberries.

4 Spoon the mixture into the paper cases. Bake in the preheated oven for 20 minutes, until risen and lightly browned.

5 Remove the muffins from the oven, transfer to a wire rack and leave to cool.

lemon & poppy seed muffins

makes 12

- 280 g/10 oz plain flour
- 1 tbsp baking powder
- ⅛ tsp salt
- 115 g/4 oz caster sugar
- 2 tbsp poppy seeds
- 2 eggs
- 250 ml/9 fl oz milk
- 6 tbsp sunflower oil or 85 g/ 3 oz unsalted butter, melted and cooled
- finely grated rind of 2 lemons

1 Preheat the oven to 200°C/400°F/Gas Mark 6. Put 12 paper muffin cases in a muffin tin, or put 12 double-layer paper cases on a baking tray.

2 Sift together the flour, baking powder and salt into a large bowl. Stir in the sugar and poppy seeds.

3 Lightly beat the eggs in a large jug or bowl, then beat in the milk, oil and lemon rind. Make a well in the centre of the dry ingredients and pour in the beaten liquid ingredients. Stir gently until just combined; do not over-mix.

4 Spoon the mixture into the paper cases. Bake in the preheated oven for about 20 minutes, until well risen, golden brown and firm to the touch.

5 Remove the muffins from the oven, transfer to a wire rack and leave to cool.

coconut lamingtons

makes 16

- oil or melted butter, for greasing
- 175 g/6 oz plain flour
- 1 tbsp baking powder
- 175 g/6 oz unsalted butter, softened
- 175 g/6 oz caster sugar
- 3 eggs, beaten
- 1 tsp vanilla extract
- 2 tbsp milk
- 2 tbsp desiccated coconut

icing & coating

- 500 g/1 lb 2 oz icing sugar
- 40 g/1½ oz cocoa powder
- 85 ml/3 fl oz boiling water
- 70 g/2½ oz unsalted butter, melted
- 250 g/9 oz desiccated coconut

1 Preheat the oven to 180°C/350°F/Gas Mark 4. Grease and line a 23-cm/9-inch square cake tin.

2 Sift the flour and baking powder into a large bowl and add the butter, caster sugar, eggs and vanilla extract. Beat well until the mixture is smooth, then stir in the milk and coconut.

3 Spoon the mixture into the prepared tin and smooth the surface with a palette knife. Bake in the preheated oven for 30–35 minutes, or until risen, firm and golden brown.

4 Leave to cool in the tin for 10 minutes, then turn out and finish cooling on a wire rack. When the cake is cold, cut into 16 squares with a sharp knife.

5 For the icing, sift the icing sugar and cocoa into a bowl. Add the water and butter and stir until smooth. Spread out the coconut on a large plate. Dip each piece of sponge cake into the icing, holding with 2 forks to coat evenly, then toss in coconut to cover.

6 Place on a sheet of baking paper and leave to set.

chocolate madeleines

makes 30

- 3 eggs
- 1 egg yolk
- 1 tsp vanilla extract
- 140 g/5 oz caster sugar
- 115 g/4 oz plain flour
- 25 g/1 oz cocoa powder
- 1 tsp baking powder
- 140 g/5 oz unsalted butter, melted and cooled, plus extra for greasing
- icing sugar, for dusting

1 Preheat the oven to 190°C/375°F/Gas Mark 5. Lightly grease 30 holes in 2–3 standard-sized madeleine tins.

2 Place the eggs, egg yolk, vanilla extract and caster sugar in a large bowl and beat with an electric mixer until very pale and thick.

3 Sift in the flour, cocoa and baking powder and fold in lightly and evenly using a metal spoon. Fold in the melted butter evenly.

4 Spoon the mixture into the prepared tins, filling to about three-quarters full. Bake in the preheated oven for 8–10 minutes, until risen and springy to the touch.

5 Remove the cakes carefully from the tins and cool on a wire rack. Lightly dust with icing sugar before serving. They are best eaten the day they are made.

cherry & sultana scones

makes 8
- 225 g/8 oz self-raising flour, plus extra for dusting
- 1 tbsp caster sugar
- pinch of salt
- 85 g/3 oz unsalted butter, cut into small pieces, plus extra for greasing
- 3 tbsp glacé cherries, chopped
- 3 tbsp sultanas
- 1 egg, lightly beaten
- 3 tbsp milk

1 Preheat the oven to 220°C/425°F/Gas Mark 7. Grease and line a baking tray.

2 Sift the flour, sugar and salt into a mixing bowl and rub in the butter with your fingertips until the mixture resembles breadcrumbs.

3 Stir in the glacé cherries and sultanas. Add the egg and 2 tablespoons of the milk. Mix well together to form a soft dough.

4 On a lightly floured work surface, roll out the dough to a thickness of 2 cm/¾ inch and cut out 8 rounds using a 5-cm/2-inch biscuit cutter.

5 Place the scones on the prepared baking tray and brush the tops with the remaining milk.

6 Bake in the preheated oven for 8–10 minutes, or until the scones are golden brown. Transfer to a wire rack to cool completely.

Mmmm...

rock cakes

makes about 8

- 225 g/8 oz plain flour
- 2 tsp baking powder
- 115 g/4 oz unsalted butter, plus extra for greasing
- 85 g/3 oz soft light brown sugar
- 85 g/3 oz mixed dried fruit
- finely grated rind of 1 lemon
- 1 egg
- 1–2 tbsp milk
- 2 tsp demerara sugar

1 Preheat the oven to 200°C/400°F/Gas Mark 6. Lightly grease 2 baking trays.

2 Sift the flour and baking powder into a large bowl. Add the butter and rub it in with your fingertips until the mixture resembles breadcrumbs. Stir in the brown sugar, mixed dried fruit and lemon rind.

3 Place the egg and a tablespoon of the milk in a bowl and beat lightly, then stir into the flour mixture, adding a little more milk if necessary, until it starts to bind together to form a moist but firm dough. Spoon small heaps of the mixture onto the prepared baking trays. Sprinkle with the demerara sugar.

4 Bake in the preheated oven for 15–20 minutes, or until golden brown and firm. Use a palette knife to transfer the cakes to a wire rack to cool.

apple turnovers

makes 8
- 250 g/9 oz ready-made puff pastry
- plain flour, for dusting
- milk, for glazing

filling
- 450 g/1 lb cooking apples, peeled, cored and chopped
- grated rind of 1 lemon (optional)
- pinch of ground cloves (optional)
- 3 tbsp granulated sugar

orange sugar
- 1 tbsp granulated sugar
- finely grated rind of 1 orange

orange cream
- 250 ml/9 fl oz double cream
- grated rind of 1 orange
- juice of ½ orange
- icing sugar, to taste

1 For the filling, mix together the apples, lemon rind and ground cloves, if using, but do not add the sugar until the last minute. For the orange sugar, mix together the granulated sugar and orange rind.

2 Preheat the oven to 220°C/425°F/Gas Mark 7. Roll the pastry out on a floured work surface into a rectangle measuring 60 x 30 cm/24 x 12 inches. Cut in half lengthways, then across into 4 to make 8 x 15-cm/6-inch squares.

3 Mix the granulated sugar into the apple filling. Brush each square lightly with milk and place a little of the apple filling in the centre. Fold a corner over diagonally to meet the opposite corner, making a triangular turnover, and press the edges together very firmly. Place on a baking tray. Repeat with the remaining squares.

4 Brush the turnovers with milk and sprinkle with the orange sugar. Bake in the preheated oven for 15–20 minutes, until puffed and well browned. Transfer to a wire rack to cool.

5 For the orange cream, whip the cream with the orange rind and juice until thick. Add a little icing sugar to taste and whip again until the cream just holds soft peaks. Serve the turnovers warm with the orange cream.

double chocolate swirls

makes 24
- 600 g/1 lb 5 oz strong white flour, plus extra for dusting
- 7 g/¼ oz easy-blend dried yeast
- 115 g/4 oz caster sugar
- ½ tsp salt
- 1 tsp ground cinnamon
- 85 g/3 oz unsalted butter
- 2 large eggs, beaten, plus extra for glazing
- 300 ml/10 fl oz milk
- oil, for greasing

filling
- 6 tbsp chocolate hazelnut spread
- 200 g/7 oz milk chocolate, chopped

1 Mix together the flour, yeast, sugar, salt and cinnamon in a large bowl.

2 Melt the butter in a heatproof bowl set over a saucepan of gently simmering water, then leave to cool slightly. Whisk in the eggs and milk. Pour into the flour mixture and mix well to form a dough.

3 Turn out onto a floured work surface and knead for 10 minutes, until smooth. Put into a large floured bowl, cover with clingfilm and put in a warm place for 1½–2 hours.

4 When you are ready to make the buns, take the dough from the bowl and punch down. Preheat the oven to 220°C/425°F/Gas Mark 7. Lightly oil 2 baking trays.

5 Divide the dough into 4 pieces and roll each piece into a rectangle about 2.5 cm/1 inch thick. Spread each rectangle with some of the chocolate hazelnut spread and scatter over a little chopped chocolate. Roll up each piece from 1 of the long edges, then cut into 6 pieces. Place each swirl, cut-side down, on 1 of the prepared baking trays and brush with the beaten egg. Bake in the preheated oven for 12–15 minutes, until golden brown. Serve warm.

raspberry chocolate éclairs

makes about 12
choux pastry
- 55 g/2 oz butter
- 150 ml/5 fl oz water
- 70 g/2½ oz plain flour, sifted
- 2 eggs, beaten

filling & topping
- 175 ml/6 fl oz double cream
- 1 tbsp icing sugar
- 175 g/6 oz fresh raspberries
- 85 g/3 oz plain chocolate, broken into pieces

1 Preheat the oven to 220°C/425°F/Gas Mark 7. Dampen a baking tray with water.

2 To make the choux pastry, place the butter and water in a heavy-based saucepan and bring to the boil over a low heat. Add the flour, all at once, and beat thoroughly until the mixture leaves the side of the saucepan. Leave to cool slightly, then vigorously beat in the eggs, a little at a time.

3 Spoon the mixture into a piping bag fitted with a 1-cm/½-inch plain nozzle and pipe 7.5-cm/3-inch lengths onto the prepared baking tray. Bake in the preheated oven for 10 minutes, then reduce the oven temperature to 190°C/375°F/Gas Mark 5 and bake for an additional 20 minutes, or until crisp and golden brown. Split the side of each éclair to let the steam escape, then transfer to a wire rack to cool completely.

4 To make the filling, place the cream and icing sugar in a bowl and whip until thick. Split the éclairs lengthways and spoon in the cream mixture. Place a few raspberries in each éclair.

5 Melt the chocolate in a heatproof bowl set over a saucepan of gently simmering water. Spread a little on top of each éclair. Leave to set, then serve.

chocolate nut brownies

makes 16
- groundnut oil, for oiling
- 225 g/8 oz plain chocolate
- 175 g/6 oz soft margarine
- 3 large eggs
- 100 g/3½ oz caster sugar
- 175 g/6 oz self-raising flour
- 100 g/3½ oz walnuts or blanched hazelnuts, chopped
- 50 g/1¾ oz milk chocolate chips

1 Preheat the oven to 180°C/350°F/Gas Mark 4. Lightly oil a 25-cm/10-inch square cake tin.

2 Place the chocolate and margarine in a heatproof bowl set over a saucepan of gently simmering water and heat until melted. Remove the bowl from the saucepan and stir well to combine the chocolate and margarine.

3 Meanwhile, beat the eggs and sugar together in a bowl until pale and creamy. Stir in the melted chocolate mixture, then add the flour, walnuts and chocolate chips. Mix together well.

4 Spoon the mixture into the prepared tin. Bake in the preheated oven for 30 minutes, or until the top is set and the centre is still slightly sticky. Leave to cool in the tin, then lift out and cut into squares.

chocolate chip & walnut slices

makes 18

- 115 g/4 oz walnut pieces
- 225 g/8 oz unsalted butter, plus extra for greasing
- 175 g/6 oz caster sugar
- a few drops of vanilla extract
- 225 g/8 oz plain flour
- 200 g/7 oz plain chocolate chips

1 Preheat the oven to 180°C/350°F/Gas Mark 4. Grease and line a 20 x 30-cm/8 x 12-inch Swiss roll tin.

2 Coarsely chop the walnut pieces to about the same size as the chocolate chips and set aside.

3 Beat the butter and sugar together until pale and fluffy. Add the vanilla extract, then stir in the flour. Stir in the reserved walnuts and the chocolate chips. Press the mixture into the prepared tin.

4 Bake in the preheated oven for 20–25 minutes, until golden brown. Leave to cool in the tin, then cut into slices.

coconut paradise slices

makes 16

- 200 g/7 oz plain chocolate, broken into pieces
- 100 g/3½ oz unsalted butter, plus extra for greasing
- 200 g/7 oz caster sugar
- 2 large eggs, lightly beaten
- 200 g/7 oz desiccated coconut
- 100 g/3½ oz sultanas
- 100 g/3½ oz glacé cherries

1 Grease and line a 23-cm/9-inch square cake tin. Place the chocolate in a heatproof bowl set over a saucepan of gently simmering water and heat until melted. Remove from the heat and stir until smooth. Pour into the prepared tin and leave to set for about 1 hour.

2 Preheat the oven to 180°C/350°F/Gas Mark 4. Place the butter and sugar in a large bowl and whisk together until pale and creamy. Gradually whisk in the eggs, then add the coconut, sultanas and glacé cherries and stir together until combined. Spoon the mixture into the tin on top of the chocolate and spread out evenly.

3 Bake in the preheated oven for 30–35 minutes, or until golden brown. Leave to cool in the tin, then turn out and cut into slices to serve.

date & nut crumble bars

makes 12

- 250 g/9 oz unsalted butter, plus extra for greasing
- 225 g/8 oz plain flour
- 200 g/7 oz porridge oats
- 175 g/6 oz light muscovado sugar
- finely grated rind and juice of 1 lemon
- 100 g/3½ oz chopped mixed nuts
- 250 g/9 oz ready-to-eat stoned dates, chopped
- ½ tsp ground mixed spice

1 Preheat the oven to 190°C/375°F/Gas Mark 5. Lightly grease a 31 x 17-cm/12½ x 6½-inch cake tin.

2 Place the butter in a mixing bowl with the flour and oats, then rub in the butter with your fingertips to make coarse crumbs. Stir in 150 g/5½ oz of the sugar, the lemon rind and half the chopped nuts, mixing to a crumbly dough.

3 Tip about two thirds of the mixture into the prepared tin and press with your knuckles to spread evenly over the base. Mix the remaining dough with the remaining nuts, stirring to make a crumbly mixture.

4 Place the dates in a small saucepan with the remaining sugar, the lemon juice and the mixed spice. Stir until boiling, then simmer for 1–2 minutes, until most of the juices are absorbed. Spread over the dough in the tin, then top with the crumble mixture, pressing down lightly.

5 Bake in the preheated oven for 35–40 minutes, until golden brown. Leave to cool for about 30 minutes, then cut into bars and leave to cool completely in the tin.

orange flapjack fingers

makes 18

- 175 g/6 oz unsalted butter, plus extra for greasing
- 150 g/5½ oz golden syrup
- 70 g/2½ oz demerara sugar
- 200 g/7 oz porridge oats
- 70 g/2½ oz wholemeal plain flour
- 70 g/2½ oz raisins or sultanas
- finely grated rind of 1 large orange

1 Preheat the oven to 180°C/375°F/Gas Mark 4. Grease and line a 25 x 20-cm/10 x 8-inch baking tin.

2 Put the butter, golden syrup and sugar into a saucepan over a high heat and stir until the butter and syrup have melted and the sugar has dissolved, then bring to the boil without stirring.

3 Put the oats, flour, raisins and orange rind into a large mixing bowl. Pour in the butter mixture and stir all the ingredients together. Tip the mixture into the prepared tin and use the back of a wooden spoon to spread it evenly over the base of the tin and into the corners.

4 Bake in the preheated oven for 25–30 minutes, until the flapjack mixture has set. Leave to cool completely in the tin.

5 When cool, invert the tin onto a chopping board. Using a serrated knife, cut in half lengthways, then cut each half into thick fingers.

cranberry & pecan slices

makes 12

- unsalted butter, for greasing
- 250 g/9 oz no-added-sugar muesli
- 75 g/2¾ oz dried cranberries
- 50 g/1¾ oz pecan nuts, chopped
- 100 g/3½ oz demerara sugar
- 3 tbsp honey
- 2 egg whites, lightly beaten
- 175 ml/6 fl oz apple juice

1 Preheat the oven to 180°C/350°F/Gas Mark 4. Grease and line a 22-cm/8½-inch square cake tin.

2 Mix the muesli, cranberries, pecan nuts and sugar together in a large bowl.

3 Warm the honey in a saucepan over a low heat, then stir into the muesli mixture. Stir in the egg whites and apple juice and mix well.

4 Spoon the mixture into the prepared tin and press down firmly. Bake in the preheated oven for 30 minutes, until golden brown. Leave to cool in the tin, then cut into 12 slices.

Mmmm...
cookies

double chocolate cookies

makes about 30

- 225 g/8 oz unsalted butter, softened
- 140 g/5 oz caster sugar
- 1 egg yolk, lightly beaten
- 2 tsp vanilla extract
- 250 g/9 oz plain flour
- 25 g/1 oz cocoa powder
- pinch of salt
- 350 g/12 oz plain chocolate, chopped
- 55 g/2 oz dried cherries

1 Preheat the oven to 190°C/375°F/Gas Mark 5. Line 2 large baking trays with baking paper.

2 Place the butter and sugar in a large bowl and beat together until light and fluffy, then beat in the egg yolk and vanilla extract. Sift the flour, cocoa and salt into the mixture, add the chopped chocolate and dried cherries and stir until combined.

3 Scoop up tablespoons of the mixture and shape into balls. Place them on the prepared baking trays, spaced well apart, and flatten slightly.

4 Bake in the preheated oven for 12–15 minutes. Leave to cool on the baking trays for 5–10 minutes, then transfer the cookies to wire racks to cool completely.

chewy oat biscuits

makes 24

- 125 g/4½ oz unsalted butter, softened
- 200 g/7 oz caster sugar
- 1 large egg
- ¼ tsp vanilla extract
- 115 g/4 oz white plain flour
- 115 g/4 oz wholemeal plain flour
- ¾ tsp bicarbonate of soda
- pinch of salt
- 40 g/1½ oz porridge oats
- 100 g/3½ oz raisins or sultanas

1 Preheat the oven to 180°C/350°F/Gas Mark 4.

2 Put the butter and sugar into a large bowl and beat until light and fluffy. Beat in the egg and vanilla extract. Sift in the flours, bicarbonate of soda and salt, adding any bran left in the sieve. Add the oats and raisins and stir well.

3 Shape the dough into 24 equal-sized balls. Place them on baking trays, spaced well apart.

4 Bake in the preheated oven for 12–14 minutes, until golden brown at the edges. Transfer to a wire rack to cool.

crunchy peanut biscuits

makes 20

- 125 g/4½ oz unsalted butter, softened, plus extra for greasing
- 150 g/5½ oz chunky peanut butter
- 225 g/8 oz granulated sugar
- 1 egg, lightly beaten
- 150 g/5½ oz plain flour
- ½ tsp baking powder
- pinch of salt
- 75 g/2¾ oz unsalted peanuts, chopped

1 Lightly grease 2 large baking trays.

2 Place the butter and peanut butter in a large bowl and beat together. Gradually add the sugar and beat together well. Add the egg, a little at a time, until it is combined.

3 Sift the flour, baking powder and salt into the peanut butter mixture. Add the peanuts and bring all of the ingredients together to form a soft dough. Wrap the dough in clingfilm and chill in the refrigerator for 30 minutes.

4 Preheat the oven to 190°C/375°F/Gas Mark 5. Form the dough into 20 equal-sized balls and place them on the prepared baking trays, about 5 cm/2 inches apart. Flatten them slightly with your hand.

5 Bake in the preheated oven for 15 minutes, or until golden brown. Transfer to wire racks to cool.

coconut & cranberry cookies

makes about 30

- 225 g/8 oz unsalted butter, softened
- 140 g/5 oz caster sugar
- 1 egg yolk, lightly beaten
- 2 tsp vanilla extract
- 280 g/10 oz plain flour
- pinch of salt
- 40 g/1½ oz desiccated coconut
- 60 g/2¼ oz dried cranberries

1 Preheat the oven to 190°C/375°F/Gas Mark 5. Line 2 large baking trays with baking paper.

2 Place the butter and sugar in a large bowl and beat together until light and fluffy, then beat in the egg yolk and vanilla extract. Sift together the flour and salt into the mixture, add the coconut and cranberries and stir until combined.

3 Scoop up tablespoons of the dough and place in mounds on the prepared baking trays, spaced well apart.

4 Bake in the preheated oven for 12–15 minutes, or until golden brown. Leave to cool on the baking trays for 5–10 minutes, then transfer the cookies to wire racks to cool completely.

lemon chocolate pinwheels

makes 40

- 175 g/6 oz unsalted butter, softened, plus extra for greasing
- 250 g/9 oz caster sugar
- 1 egg, beaten
- 350 g/12 oz plain flour, plus extra for dusting
- 25 g/1 oz plain chocolate, broken into pieces
- grated rind of 1 lemon

1 Grease and flour several baking trays.

2 In a large mixing bowl, cream together the butter and sugar until light and fluffy. Gradually add the egg to the creamed mixture, beating well after each addition. Sift the flour into the mixture and mix thoroughly until a soft dough forms.

3 Transfer half of the dough to a separate bowl. Put the chocolate in a heatproof bowl set over a saucepan of gently simmering water until melted. Leave to cool slightly. Beat into half of the dough. Stir the lemon rind into the other half of the dough.

4 On a lightly floured work surface, roll out the dough to form 2 rectangles. Lay the lemon dough on top of the chocolate dough. Roll up tightly, using a sheet of baking paper to guide you. Chill in the refrigerator for 1 hour.

5 Preheat the oven to 190°C/375°F/Gas Mark 5. Cut the roll into 40 slices, place on the prepared baking trays and bake in the preheated oven for 10–12 minutes, or until lightly golden. Transfer to a wire rack and leave to cool completely.

crunchy seed & spice cookies

makes about 22

- 85 g/3 oz unsalted butter, plus extra for greasing
- 85 g/3 oz light muscovado sugar
- 1 egg, beaten
- 225 g/8 oz plain flour
- 1 tsp caraway seeds
- 1 tsp ground nutmeg
- 55 g/2 oz sunflower seeds

1 Preheat the oven to 200°C/400°F/Gas Mark 6. Lightly grease 2 baking trays.

2 Using an electric mixer, cream together the butter and sugar until soft and fluffy. Add the egg and beat thoroughly, then stir in the flour, caraway seeds and nutmeg, mixing evenly to a fairly stiff dough.

3 Roll heaped teaspoonfuls of dough into walnut-sized balls with your hands. Toss them roughly in the sunflower seeds to coat lightly, then arrange on the prepared baking trays and press lightly with your fingers to flatten slightly.

4 Bake in the preheated oven for 12–15 minutes, or until golden brown. Transfer to a wire rack to cool.

thumbprint cookies

makes about 36

- 115 g/4 oz unsalted butter, softened
- 125 g/4½ oz caster sugar
- 1 large egg, separated
- 1 tsp vanilla extract
- 175 g/6 oz plain flour
- pinch of salt
- 25 g/1 oz ground almonds
- 100 g/3½ oz raspberry jam

1 Preheat the oven to 180°C/350°F/Gas Mark 4. Line 2 large baking trays with baking paper.

2 Place the butter and 100 g/3½ oz of the sugar in a large bowl and beat together until light and fluffy. Add the egg yolk and vanilla extract and beat well to combine. Sift in the flour and salt and mix well.

3 Mix the remaining sugar and the ground almonds together and spread out on a plate. Lightly whisk the egg white in a separate bowl. Roll walnut-sized pieces of dough into balls, then dip each ball into the egg white and roll in the almond sugar. Place the balls on the prepared baking trays and make a deep indentation in each cookie with your thumb.

4 Bake in the preheated oven for 10 minutes. Remove from the oven, press down again on each indentation and fill it with a little of the jam. Bake for a further 10–12 minutes, or until the cookies are golden brown, turning the baking trays once. Transfer to wire racks to cool.

cherry & chocolate diamonds

makes about 30

- 225 g/8 oz unsalted butter, softened
- 140 g/5 oz caster sugar
- 1 egg yolk, lightly beaten
- 2 tsp vanilla extract
- 280 g/10 oz plain flour
- pinch of salt
- 55 g/2 oz glacé cherries, finely chopped
- 55 g/2 oz milk chocolate chips

1 Place the butter and sugar in a large bowl and beat together until light and fluffy, then beat in the egg yolk and vanilla extract. Sift together the flour and salt into the mixture, add the glacé cherries and chocolate chips and stir until thoroughly combined. Halve the dough and shape into balls, then wrap in clingfilm and chill in the refrigerator for 30–60 minutes.

2 Preheat the oven to 190°C/375°F/Gas Mark 5. Line 2 large baking trays with baking paper.

3 Unwrap the dough and roll out between 2 sheets of baking paper to about 3 mm/⅛ inch thick. Cut out cookies with a diamond-shaped cutter and place them on the prepared baking trays.

4 Bake in the preheated oven for 10–15 minutes, or until light golden brown. Leave to cool on the baking trays for 5–10 minutes, then transfer the cookies to wire racks to cool completely.

tangy lemon jumbles

makes 40

- groundnut oil, for oiling
- 100 g/3½ oz unsalted butter, softened
- 125 g/4½ oz caster sugar
- finely grated rind of 1 lemon
- 1 large egg, lightly beaten
- 4 tbsp lemon juice
- 350 g/12 oz plain flour, plus extra for dusting
- 1 tsp baking powder
- 1 tbsp milk

1 Preheat the oven to 160°C/325°F/Gas Mark 3. Oil 2 large baking trays.

2 Place the butter, caster sugar and lemon rind in a large bowl and beat together until light and fluffy. Alternately add the egg and lemon juice to the mixture, beating well between each addition. Sift in the flour and baking powder and mix well, then add the milk to form a smooth dough.

3 Turn the dough out onto a floured work surface and divide into 40 pieces. Roll each piece into a sausage, then form into an S-shape and place on the prepared baking trays. Bake in the preheated oven for 15–20 minutes. Transfer to a wire rack to cool.

jam sandwich biscuits

makes 24

- 225 g/8 oz unsalted butter, softened
- 100 g/3½ oz caster sugar
- 200 g/7 oz plain flour, plus extra for dusting
- pinch of salt
- 100 g/3½ oz ground almonds
- 55 g/2 oz raspberry jam
- 55 g/2 oz apricot jam
- 2 tbsp icing sugar

1 Place the butter and caster sugar in a large bowl and beat together until light and fluffy. Add the flour, salt and ground almonds and bring together to form a soft dough. Wrap the dough in clingfilm and chill in the refrigerator for 2 hours.

2 Preheat the oven to 150°C/300°F/Gas Mark 2.

3 Roll the dough out on a floured work surface to about 5 mm/¼ inch thick. Using a 7-cm/2¾-inch biscuit cutter dipped in flour, cut out 48 rounds. Use a small round biscuit cutter to cut out the centre from 24 of the rounds and place the biscuits on 2 large baking trays. Bake in the preheated oven for 25–30 minutes, or until golden. Transfer to a wire rack to cool completely.

4 Spoon the raspberry jam onto 12 of the complete biscuits. Spoon the apricot jam onto the remaining 12. Sift the icing sugar over the cut-out biscuits and use these to cover the jam-topped biscuits, pressing down gently.

crunchy nut & honey sandwiches

makes about 30

- 300 g/10½ oz unsalted butter, softened
- 140 g/5 oz caster sugar
- 1 egg yolk, lightly beaten
- 2 tsp vanilla extract
- 280 g/10 oz plain flour
- pinch of salt
- 40 g/1½ oz macadamia nuts, cashew nuts or pine kernels, chopped
- 85 g/3 oz icing sugar
- 85 g/3 oz set honey

1 Preheat the oven to 190°C/375°F/Gas Mark 5. Line 2 large baking trays with baking paper.

2 Place 225 g/8 oz of the butter and the caster sugar in a large bowl and beat together until light and fluffy, then beat in the egg yolk and vanilla extract. Sift the flour and salt into the mixture and stir until combined.

3 Scoop up tablespoons of the dough and roll into balls. Place half of them on 1 of the prepared baking trays, spaced well apart, and flatten gently. Spread out the nuts in a shallow dish and dip 1 side of the remaining dough balls into them, then place on the other baking tray, nut-side uppermost, and flatten gently.

4 Bake in the preheated oven for 10–15 minutes, or until light golden brown. Leave to cool on the baking trays for 5–10 minutes, then transfer the cookies to wire racks to cool completely.

5 Place the remaining butter, the icing sugar and honey in a bowl and beat together until creamy. Spread the honey mixture over the plain cookies and top with the nut-coated cookies.

shortbread

makes 8

- 175 g/6 oz plain flour, plus extra for dusting
- pinch of salt
- 55 g/2 oz caster sugar, plus extra for sprinkling
- 115 g/4 oz unsalted butter, cut into small pieces, plus extra for greasing

1 Preheat the oven to 150°C/300°F/Gas Mark 2. Grease a 20-cm/8-inch fluted tart tin.

2 Mix together the flour, salt and sugar. Rub the butter into the dry ingredients. Continue to work the mixture until it forms a soft dough. Make sure you do not overwork the shortbread or it will be tough, not crumbly as it should be.

3 Lightly press the dough into the cake tin. If you don't have a fluted tin, roll out the dough on a lightly floured work surface, place on a baking tray and pinch the edges to form a scalloped pattern.

4 Mark into 8 pieces with a knife. Prick all over with a fork and bake in the preheated oven for 45–50 minutes, until the shortbread is firm and just coloured.

5 Leave to cool in the tin and sprinkle with sugar. Cut into portions and transfer to a wire rack.

coconut macaroons

makes 8
- 2 large egg whites
- 115 g/4 oz caster sugar
- 150 g/5½ oz desiccated coconut
- 8 glacé cherries

1 Preheat the oven to 180°C/350°F/Gas Mark 4. Line 2 large baking trays with rice paper.

2 Place the egg whites in a large bowl and whisk until soft peaks form and they hold their shape but are not dry. Add the sugar to the egg whites and, using a large metal spoon, fold in until incorporated. Add the coconut and fold into the mixture.

3 Place 4 heaped tablespoons of the mixture onto each of the prepared baking trays and place a cherry on top of each macaroon.

4 Bake in the preheated oven for 15–20 minutes, or until light golden brown around the edges. Transfer to a wire rack to cool completely.

cherry garlands

makes about 30

- 150 g/5½ oz unsalted butter, softened
- 50 g/1¾ oz icing sugar
- ½ tsp vanilla extract
- 150 g/5½ oz plain flour
- pinch of salt
- 70 g/2½ oz glacé cherries, finely chopped

1 Preheat the oven to 190°C/375°F/Gas Mark 5.

2 Place the butter and sugar in a large bowl and beat together until light and fluffy. Add the vanilla extract and beat until combined. Sift in the flour and salt in batches, mixing well between each addition. Add the cherries and mix well.

3 Spoon the mixture into a piping bag fitted with a 2.5-cm/1-inch star nozzle and pipe rings onto 2 large baking trays.

4 Bake in the preheated oven for 8–10 minutes, or until light golden. Transfer to a wire rack to cool.

melting moments

makes 64

- 350 g / 12 oz unsalted butter, softened
- 85 g / 3 oz icing sugar
- ½ tsp vanilla extract
- 300 g / 10½ oz plain flour
- 50 g / 1¾ oz cornflour

1 Preheat the oven to 180°C/350°F/Gas Mark 4. Line 2 large baking trays with baking paper.

2 Place the butter and icing sugar in a large bowl and beat together until light and fluffy, then beat in the vanilla extract. Sift in the flour and cornflour and mix thoroughly.

3 Spoon the mixture into a piping bag fitted with a large star nozzle and pipe 32 cookies onto each prepared baking tray, spaced well apart.

4 Bake in the preheated oven for 15–20 minutes, or until golden brown. Leave to cool on the baking trays.

chocolate-dipped viennese fingers

makes about 16

- 100 g/3½ oz unsalted butter, plus extra for greasing
- 25 g/1 oz golden caster sugar
- ½ tsp vanilla extract
- 100 g/3½ oz self-raising flour
- 100 g/3½ oz plain chocolate

1 Preheat the oven to 160°C/325°F/Gas Mark 3. Lightly grease 2 baking trays.

2 Place the butter, sugar and vanilla extract in a bowl and cream together until pale and fluffy. Stir in the flour, mixing evenly to a fairly stiff dough.

3 Place the mixture in a piping bag fitted with a large star nozzle and pipe about 16 fingers, each 6 cm/2½ inches long, onto the prepared baking trays.

4 Bake in the preheated oven for 10–15 minutes, until pale golden. Leave to cool on the baking trays for 2–3 minutes, then lift carefully onto a wire rack with a palette knife to finish cooling.

5 Place the chocolate in a small heatproof bowl set over a pan of gently simmering water until melted. Remove from the heat. Dip the ends of each biscuit into the chocolate to coat, then place on a sheet of baking paper and leave to set.

zesty almond biscotti

makes about 20

- butter, for greasing
- 280 g/10 oz plain flour, plus extra for dusting
- 1 tsp baking powder
- 150 g/5½ oz caster sugar
- 85 g/3 oz blanched almonds
- 2 large eggs, lightly beaten
- finely grated rind and juice of 1 lemon

1 Preheat the oven to 180°C/350°F/Gas Mark 4. Grease a large baking tray.

2 Sift the flour and baking powder into a large bowl. Add the sugar, almonds, eggs, lemon rind and juice to the flour and mix together to form a soft dough. Turn the dough onto a lightly floured work surface and, with floured hands, knead for 2–3 minutes, or until smooth.

3 Divide the dough in half and shape each portion into a log shape measuring about 4 cm/1½ inches in diameter. Place the logs on the prepared baking tray and flatten until each is about 2.5 cm/1 inch thick.

4 Bake in the preheated oven for 25 minutes, or until light golden brown. Remove from the oven and leave to cool for 15 minutes. Reduce the oven temperature to 150°C/300°F/Gas Mark 2.

5 Using a serrated knife, cut the baked dough into 1 cm/½ inch thick slices and place, cut-side down, on ungreased baking trays. Bake for a further 10 minutes. Turn and bake for 10–15 minutes, or until golden brown and crisp. Transfer to a wire rack and leave to cool and harden.

pistachio &
almond tuiles

makes about 12

- 1 egg white
- 55 g/2 oz golden caster sugar
- 25 g/1 oz plain flour
- 25 g/1 oz pistachio nuts, finely chopped
- 25 g/1 oz ground almonds
- ½ tsp almond extract
- 40 g/1½ oz unsalted butter, melted and cooled

1 Preheat the oven to 160°C/325°F/Gas Mark 3. Line 2 baking trays with baking paper.

2 Whisk the egg white lightly with the sugar, then stir in the flour, pistachios, ground almonds, almond extract and butter, mixing to a soft paste.

3 Place walnut-sized spoonfuls of the mixture on the prepared baking trays and use the back of the spoon to spread as thinly as possible. Bake in the preheated oven for 10–15 minutes, until pale golden.

4 Quickly lift each biscuit with a palette knife and place over the side of a rolling pin to shape into a curve. When set, transfer to a wire rack to cool.

brandy snaps

makes about 20

- 85 g/3 oz unsalted butter
- 85 g/3 oz golden caster sugar
- 3 tbsp golden syrup
- 85 g/3 oz plain flour
- 1 tsp ground ginger
- 1 tbsp brandy
- finely grated rind of ½ lemon

filling

- 150 ml/5 fl oz double cream or whipping cream
- 1 tbsp brandy (optional)
- 1 tbsp icing sugar

1 Preheat the oven to 160°C/325°F/Gas Mark 3. Line 3 large baking trays with baking paper.

2 Place the butter, caster sugar and golden syrup in a saucepan and heat gently over a low heat, stirring occasionally, until melted. Remove from the heat and leave to cool slightly. Sift the flour and ginger into the pan and beat until smooth, then stir in the brandy and lemon rind.

3 Drop small spoonfuls of the mixture onto the prepared baking trays, spaced well apart. Place 1 baking tray at a time in the preheated oven for 10–12 minutes, or until golden brown.

4 Remove the first baking tray from the oven and leave to cool for about 30 seconds, then lift each brandy snap with a palette knife and wrap around the handle of a wooden spoon. If the brandy snaps start to become too firm to wrap, return them to the oven for about 30 seconds to soften again. When firm, remove from the spoon handles and finish cooling on a wire rack. Repeat with the remaining baking trays.

5 For the filling, whip the cream with the brandy, if using, and icing sugar until thick. Just before serving, pipe a little of the cream mixture into each end of the brandy snaps.

chocolate-dipped finger rolls

makes about 35

- 250 g/9 oz icing sugar
- 125 g/4½ oz plain flour
- pinch of salt
- 6 large egg whites
- 1 tbsp double cream
- 1 tsp vanilla extract
- 125 g/4½ oz unsalted butter, melted and cooled
- 125 g/4½ oz plain chocolate, chopped

1 Sift the icing sugar, flour and salt into a large bowl. Lightly whisk the egg whites in a separate bowl, stir in the cream, vanilla extract and butter, then pour into the dry ingredients and mix until smooth. Cover and chill overnight in the refrigerator.

2 Preheat the oven to 200°C/400°F/Gas Mark 6.

3 Spoon 4 tablespoons of the batter onto a large baking tray. Using the back of a spoon, spread thinly into ovals 13 cm/5 inches long, spaced well apart. Bake in the preheated oven for 5–6 minutes, or until just browning at the edges. Prepare the second batch while the first batch is cooking.

4 Using a palette knife, take a cookie and roll around the handle of the wooden spoon to make a cigarette shape. Transfer to a wire rack to cool and repeat with the remaining cookies. Repeat until all the batter is used.

5 When the finger rolls are cold, place the chocolate in a heatproof bowl set over a saucepan of gently simmering water and heat until melted. Dip 1 end of each roll into the chocolate, then place on a wire rack to set, leaving the chocolate end hanging over the edge.

Mmmm...
desserts

white chocolate coffee gateau

serves 8–10

- 40 g/1½ oz unsalted butter, plus extra for greasing
- 85 g/3 oz white chocolate, broken into pieces
- 125 g/4½ oz caster sugar
- 4 large eggs, beaten
- 2 tbsp very strong black coffee
- 1 tsp vanilla extract
- 125 g/4½ oz plain flour
- white chocolate curls, to decorate

frosting

- 175 g/6 oz white chocolate, broken into pieces
- 85 g/3 oz unsalted butter
- 125 g/4½ oz crème fraîche
- 125 g/4½ oz icing sugar, sifted
- 1 tbsp coffee liqueur or very strong black coffee

1 Preheat the oven to 180°C/350°F/Gas Mark 4. Grease and base-line 2 x 20-cm/8-inch sandwich cake tins.

2 Place the butter and chocolate in a heatproof bowl set over a saucepan of hot water and leave on a very low heat until just melted. Stir to mix lightly, then remove from the heat.

3 Place the caster sugar, eggs, coffee and vanilla extract in a heatproof bowl set over a saucepan of hot water and whisk vigorously with an electric mixer until the mixture is pale and thick enough to leave a trail when the beaters are lifted. Remove from the heat, sift in the flour and fold in lightly. Quickly fold in the chocolate mixture, then divide between the prepared tins.

4 Bake in the preheated oven for 25–30 minutes, until risen and golden brown. Leave to cool in the tins for 2 minutes, then turn out onto a wire rack.

5 For the frosting, place the chocolate and butter in a heatproof bowl set over a saucepan of hot water and heat gently until melted. Remove from the heat and stir in the crème fraîche, icing sugar and liqueur. Chill for at least 30 minutes, until thick and glossy. Use about one third of the frosting to sandwich the cakes together. Spread the remainder over the top and sides, then decorate with chocolate curls.

chocolate & almond layer cake

serves 10-12

- 7 eggs
- 200 g/7 oz caster sugar
- 150 g/5½ oz plain flour
- 50 g/1¾ oz cocoa powder
- 50 g/1¾ oz unsalted butter, melted, plus extra for greasing

filling

- 200 g/7 oz plain chocolate, broken into pieces
- 125 g/4½ oz unsalted butter
- 50 g/1¾ oz icing sugar

to decorate

- 75 g/2¾ oz toasted flaked almonds, lightly crushed
- 40 g/1½ oz milk chocolate, grated

1 Preheat the oven to 180°C/350°F/Gas Mark 4. Grease and base-line a 23-cm/9-inch square cake tin.

2 Whisk the eggs and caster sugar in a mixing bowl with an electric mixer for about 10 minutes, or until the mixture is pale and thick enough to leave a trail when the beaters are lifted.

3 Sift together the flour and cocoa and fold half into the mixture. Drizzle over the melted butter and fold in the rest of the flour and cocoa. Pour into the prepared tin and bake in the preheated oven for 30–35 minutes, or until springy to the touch. Leave to cool slightly, then remove from the tin and transfer to a wire rack to cool completely.

4 To make the filling, place the chocolate and butter in a heatproof bowl set over a saucepan of gently simmering water until melted, then remove from the heat. Stir in the icing sugar. Leave to cool, then beat until thick enough to spread.

5 Halve the cake lengthways and cut each half into 3 layers. Sandwich the layers together with three quarters of the filling. Spread the remainder over the cake, then press the almonds onto the sides and decorate the top with the grated chocolate.

blueberry swirl gateau

serves 8–10

- oil or melted butter, for greasing
- 175 g/6 oz plain flour
- 1 tbsp baking powder
- 175 g/6 oz unsalted butter, softened
- 175 g/6 oz caster sugar
- 3 eggs, beaten
- 1 tsp orange flower water
- 2 tbsp orange juice

filling & frosting

- 200 g/7 oz full-fat soft cheese
- 100 g/3½ oz icing sugar, sifted
- 225 g/8 oz fresh blueberries

1 Preheat the oven to 160°C/325°F/Gas Mark 3. Grease and base-line 3 x 19-cm/7½-inch sandwich cake tins.

2 Sift the flour and baking powder into a large bowl and add the butter, caster sugar, eggs and orange flower water. Beat well until the mixture is smooth, then stir in the orange juice.

3 Spoon the mixture into the prepared tins and smooth the surfaces with a palette knife. Bake in the preheated oven for 20–25 minutes, or until risen, firm and golden brown.

4 Leave to cool in the tins for 2–3 minutes, then turn out and finish cooling on a wire rack.

5 For the frosting, beat together the soft cheese and icing sugar until smooth. Transfer about two thirds of the mixture to a separate bowl and stir in 140 g/ 5 oz of the blueberries, then use this to sandwich the cakes together.

6 Rub the remaining blueberries through a fine sieve to make a smooth purée. Spread the remaining frosting on top of the cake and swirl the blueberry purée through it.

pineapple hummingbird cake

serves 8–10

- oil or melted butter, for greasing
- 175 g/6 oz plain flour
- 1 tbsp baking powder
- 1 tsp ground cinnamon
- 175 g/6 oz caster sugar
- 175 ml/6 fl oz sunflower oil
- 3 eggs, beaten
- 1 tsp vanilla extract
- 55 g/2 oz pecan nuts, finely chopped
- 2 small ripe bananas, mashed
- 85 g/3 oz canned crushed pineapple, drained
- pineapple pieces and pecan nuts, to decorate

filling & frosting

- 175 g/6 oz full-fat soft cheese
- 55 g/2 oz unsalted butter, softened
- 1 tsp vanilla extract
- 400 g/14 oz icing sugar, sifted

1 Preheat the oven to 180°C/350°F/Gas Mark 4. Grease and base-line 3 x 23-cm/9-inch sandwich cake tins.

2 Sift the flour, baking powder and cinnamon into a bowl and add the caster sugar, oil, eggs and vanilla extract. Beat well until the mixture is smooth, then stir in the chopped pecan nuts, mashed bananas and crushed pineapple.

3 Divide the mixture between the prepared tins, spreading evenly. Bake in the preheated oven for 20–25 minutes, or until risen, firm and golden brown.

4 Leave to cool in the tins for 2–3 minutes, then turn out onto a wire rack to finish cooling.

5 For the frosting, beat together the soft cheese, butter, vanilla extract and icing sugar until smooth. Sandwich the cakes together with about two thirds of the frosting. Spread the remaining frosting on top, then decorate with pineapple pieces and pecan nuts.

meringue-topped coffee liqueur cake

serves 8-10
- oil or melted butter, for greasing
- 175 g/6 oz plain flour
- 1 tbsp baking powder
- 175 g/6 oz unsalted butter, softened
- 175 g/6 oz light muscovado sugar
- 3 eggs, beaten
- 1 tsp coffee extract
- 2 tbsp milk
- 3 tbsp coffee liqueur

meringue topping
- 3 egg whites
- 150 g/5½ oz caster sugar
- 1½ tsp coffee extract

1 Preheat the oven to 160°C/325°F/Gas Mark 3. Grease and line a 25-cm/10-inch round cake tin.

2 Sift the flour and baking powder into a large bowl and add the butter, muscovado sugar, eggs and coffee extract. Beat well until the mixture is smooth, then stir in the milk.

3 Spoon the mixture into the prepared tin and smooth the surface with a palette knife. Bake in the preheated oven for 40–50 minutes, or until risen, firm and golden brown.

4 Leave to cool in the tin for 2–3 minutes, then turn out onto a flameproof serving plate. Prick all over with a skewer, then sprinkle with the liqueur.

5 For the meringue topping, place the egg whites in a clean bowl and whisk with an electric mixer until holding soft peaks. Gradually add the caster sugar, whisking vigorously after each addition, then whisk in the coffee extract.

6 Spread the meringue on top of the cake. Use a chef's blowtorch to brown the meringue or place the cake under a hot grill for 2–3 minutes, or until just browned but still soft inside.

mango & ginger roulade

serves 6

- oil or melted butter, for greasing
- 150 g/5½ oz plain flour
- 1½ tsp baking powder
- 175 g/6 oz unsalted butter, softened
- 175 g/6 oz golden caster sugar, plus extra for sprinkling
- 3 eggs, beaten
- 1 tsp vanilla extract
- 2 tbsp orange juice
- 1 large ripe mango
- 3 tbsp chopped glacé ginger
- 5 tbsp crème fraîche

1 Preheat the oven to 180°C/350°F/Gas Mark 4. Grease and line a 23 x 33-cm/9 x 13-inch Swiss roll tin with the paper 1 cm/½ inch above the rim. Lay a sheet of baking paper on the work surface and sprinkle with caster sugar.

2 Sift the flour and baking powder into a large bowl and add the butter, sugar, eggs and vanilla extract. Beat well until the mixture is smooth, then beat in the orange juice.

3 Spoon the mixture into the prepared tin. Bake in the preheated oven for 15–20 minutes, or until risen, firm and golden brown.

4 Meanwhile, peel, stone and finely chop the mango. Place in a small bowl and stir in the glacé ginger.

5 When cooked, turn the sponge out onto the sugared baking paper and spread with most of the mango mixture. Roll up the sponge firmly from a short side to enclose the filling, keeping the paper around the outside to hold it in place. Lift onto a wire rack to cool, removing the paper when firm.

6 When cold, top with spoonfuls of crème fraîche and decorate with the remaining mango mixture.

sachertorte

serves 10
- 175 g/6 oz plain chocolate, broken into pieces
- 140 g/5 oz unsalted butter, plus extra for greasing
- 140 g/5 oz caster sugar
- 6 eggs, separated
- 175 g/6 oz plain flour
- fresh strawberries, to serve

icing & filling
- 225 g/8 oz plain chocolate, broken into pieces
- 5 tbsp cold strong black coffee
- 115 g/4 oz icing sugar, sifted
- 6 tbsp apricot jam, warmed

1 Preheat the oven to 150°C/300°F/Gas Mark 2. Grease and base-line a 23-cm/9-inch round springform cake tin.

2 Melt the chocolate in a heatproof bowl set over a saucepan of barely simmering water. Leave to cool slightly. Cream the butter and half the caster sugar in a bowl until pale and fluffy. Add the egg yolks and beat well. Add the melted chocolate, beating well. Sift the flour into the mixture, then fold in. Whisk the egg whites in a separate clean bowl until holding soft peaks. Add the remaining caster sugar and whisk until stiff and glossy. Fold half into the chocolate mixture, then fold in the remainder.

3 Spoon into the prepared tin and smooth the surface. Bake in the preheated oven for 1–1¼ hours, or until a skewer inserted into the centre comes out clean. Leave to cool slightly in the tin, then transfer to a wire rack and leave to cool completely.

4 To make the icing, melt 175 g/6 oz of the chocolate as above and beat in the coffee. Whisk in the icing sugar to form a thick icing. Cut the cake into 2 layers and sandwich together with the jam. Spoon over the icing and spread to coat the top and sides of the cake. Leave to set for at least 2 hours.

5 Melt the remaining chocolate and spoon into a piping bag fitted with a fine plain nozzle. Pipe 'Sachertorte' on top of the cake and leave to set. Serve with strawberries.

walnut torte

serves 8–10

- oil or melted butter, for greasing
- 175 g/6 oz plain flour
- 1 tbsp baking powder
- 175 g/6 oz unsalted butter, softened
- 175 g/6 oz golden caster sugar
- 3 eggs, beaten
- 1 tsp vanilla extract
- 2 tbsp milk
- 125 g/4½ oz walnuts, finely chopped, plus extra walnut halves to decorate
- 3 tbsp apricot jam, warmed

frosting

- 175 g/6 oz unsalted butter
- 350 g/12 oz icing sugar, sifted
- 100 ml/3½ fl oz single cream

1 Preheat the oven to 180°C/350°F/Gas Mark 4. Grease and base-line 2 x 20-cm/8-inch sandwich cake tins.

2 Sift the flour and baking powder into a large bowl and add the butter, caster sugar, eggs and vanilla extract. Beat well until the mixture is smooth, then stir in the milk and 40 g/1½ oz of the chopped walnuts.

3 Divide the mixture between the prepared tins and smooth the surfaces with a palette knife. Bake in the preheated oven for 25–30 minutes, or until risen, firm and golden brown.

4 Leave to cool in the tins for 2–3 minutes, then turn out and finish cooling on a wire rack. Slice each cake in half horizontally, to make 4 layers in total.

5 For the frosting, beat together the butter, icing sugar and cream until smooth. Spread about half the frosting over the top of 3 of the cakes and sandwich them together, placing the plain cake on top. Spread half the remaining frosting over the sides of the cake and press the remaining chopped walnuts over it.

6 Brush the apricot jam over the top of the cake. Spoon the remaining frosting into a piping bag fitted with a star nozzle and pipe swirls around the top. Decorate with walnut halves.

sticky toffee cake

serves 4
- 75 g/2¾ oz sultanas
- 150 g/5½ oz stoned dates, chopped
- 1 tsp bicarbonate of soda
- 25 g/1 oz unsalted butter, plus extra for greasing
- 200 g/7 oz soft dark brown sugar
- 2 eggs
- 200 g/7 oz self-raising flour, sifted

sticky toffee sauce
- 25 g/1 oz unsalted butter
- 175 ml/6 fl oz double cream
- 200 g/7 oz soft dark brown sugar

1 Put the sultanas, dates and bicarbonate of soda into a heatproof bowl. Cover with boiling water and leave to soak.

2 Preheat the oven to 180°C/350°F/Gas Mark 4. Grease an 18-cm/7-inch square cake tin.

3 Put the butter in a separate bowl, add the sugar and mix well. Beat in the eggs, then fold in the flour. Drain the sultanas and dates, add to the bowl and mix.

4 Spoon the mixture evenly into the prepared tin. Bake in the preheated oven for 35–40 minutes, or until a skewer inserted into the centre comes out clean.

5 About 5 minutes before the end of the cooking time, make the sauce. Melt the butter in a saucepan over a medium heat. Stir in the cream and sugar and bring to the boil, stirring constantly. Reduce the heat and simmer for 5 minutes.

6 Cut the cake into squares and turn out onto serving plates. Pour over the sauce and serve.

toffee apple upside-down cake

serves 6

- oil or melted butter, for greasing
- 175 g/6 oz plain flour
- 1 tbsp baking powder
- 175 g/6 oz unsalted butter, softened
- 175 g/6 oz caster sugar
- 3 eggs, beaten
- 1 tsp vanilla extract
- finely grated rind of 1 lemon

toffee apple topping

- 55 g/2 oz unsalted butter
- 100 g/3½ oz caster sugar
- 1 tbsp water
- 4 eating apples
- 2 tbsp lemon juice

1 Preheat the oven to 180°C/350°F/Gas Mark 4. Grease a 23-cm/9-inch round cake tin with a solid base.

2 For the toffee apple topping, place the butter and sugar in a heavy-based saucepan with the water and heat gently until melted, then bring to the boil. Reduce the heat and cook, stirring, until it turns to a deep golden caramel colour. Pour quickly into the prepared tin, tilting to cover the base evenly.

3 Peel, core and thickly slice the apples, toss with the lemon juice and spread evenly over the base of the tin.

4 Sift the flour and baking powder into a large bowl and add the butter, sugar, eggs and vanilla extract. Beat well until the mixture is smooth, then stir in the lemon rind.

5 Spoon the mixture over the apples and smooth the surface with a palette knife. Bake in the preheated oven for 40–50 minutes, or until risen and golden brown.

6 Leave to cool in the tin for 2–3 minutes, then turn out carefully onto a warmed serving plate.

new york cheesecake

serves 10

- 100 g/3½ oz unsalted butter, plus extra for greasing
- 150 g/5½ oz digestive biscuits, finely crushed
- 1 tbsp granulated sugar
- 900 g/2 lb cream cheese
- 250 g/9 oz caster sugar
- 2 tbsp plain flour
- 1 tsp vanilla extract
- finely grated rind of 1 orange
- finely grated rind of 1 lemon
- 3 eggs
- 2 egg yolks
- 300 ml/10 fl oz double cream

1 Preheat the oven to 180°C/350°F/Gas Mark 4. Grease a 23-cm/9-inch round springform cake tin.

2 Place the butter in a small saucepan over a low heat and heat until melted. Remove from the heat, stir in the crushed biscuits and granulated sugar and mix thoroughly. Press the biscuit mixture into the base of the prepared tin. Bake in the preheated oven for 10 minutes. Remove from the oven and leave to cool.

3 Increase the oven temperature to 200°C/400°F/Gas Mark 6. In a food processor, blend the cream cheese, then gradually add the caster sugar and flour and beat until smooth. Increase the speed and beat in the vanilla extract and citrus rinds, then beat in the eggs and egg yolks 1 at a time. Finally, beat in the cream.

4 Pour the filling into the cake tin. Smooth the top, transfer to the preheated oven and bake for 15 minutes, then reduce the temperature to 110°C/225°F/Gas Mark ¼ and bake for a further 30 minutes. Turn off the oven and leave the cheesecake in it for 2 hours to cool and set. Cover and refrigerate overnight.

5 Slide a knife around the edge of the tin, then remove the sides. Cut into slices and serve.

strawberry shortcake

serves 8

- 175 g/6 oz self-raising flour
- 100 g/3½ oz unsalted butter, diced and chilled, plus extra for greasing
- 75 g/2¾ oz caster sugar
- 1 egg yolk
- 1 tbsp rosewater
- 600 ml/1 pint whipping cream, lightly whipped
- 225 g/8 oz strawberries, hulled and quartered, plus a few whole strawberries to decorate
- icing sugar, for dusting

1 Preheat the oven to 190°C/375°F/Gas Mark 5. Grease and line 2 baking trays.

2 To make the shortcakes, sift the flour into a bowl. Rub in the butter with your fingertips until the mixture resembles breadcrumbs. Stir in the caster sugar, then add the egg yolk and rosewater and mix to form a soft dough.

3 Divide the dough in half. Roll out each piece into a 19-cm/7½-inch round and transfer to the prepared baking trays. Crimp the edges of the dough and prick all over with a fork.

4 Bake in the preheated oven for 15 minutes, until lightly golden. Transfer the shortcakes to a wire rack to cool.

5 Mix the cream with the strawberry quarters and spoon on top of 1 of the shortcakes. Cut the remaining shortcake round into wedges, then place on top of the cream. Dust with icing sugar and decorate with whole strawberries.

apple pie

serves 6
pastry
- 350 g/12 oz plain flour
- pinch of salt
- 85 g/3 oz unsalted butter or margarine, cut into small pieces
- 85 g/3 oz lard or white vegetable fat, cut into small pieces
- about 6 tbsp cold water
- beaten egg or milk, for glazing

filling
- 750 g–1 kg/1 lb 10 oz–2 lb 4 oz cooking apples, peeled, cored and sliced
- 125 g/4½ oz soft light brown sugar or caster sugar, plus extra for sprinkling
- ½–1 tsp ground cinnamon, mixed spice or ginger
- 1–2 tbsp water, if needed

1 To make the pastry, sift the flour and salt into a mixing bowl. Add the butter and lard and rub in with your fingertips until the mixture resembles fine breadcrumbs. Add the water and mix to form a dough. Wrap in clingfilm and chill in the refrigerator for 30 minutes.

2 Preheat the oven to 220°C/425°F/Gas Mark 7. Roll out almost two thirds of the pastry thinly and use to line a deep 23-cm/9-inch pie plate or pie tin.

3 Mix the apples with the sugar and spice and pack into the pastry case. Add the water if needed, particularly if the apples are not very juicy. Roll out the remaining pastry to form a lid. Dampen the rim of the pie with water and position the lid, pressing the edges firmly together. Trim the edges.

4 Cut the trimmings into leaves or other shapes to decorate the top of the pie. Dampen and attach. Glaze the top of the pie with beaten egg, make 1 or 2 slits in the top and place on a baking tray.

5 Bake in the preheated oven for 20 minutes, then reduce the oven temperature to 180°C/350°F/ Gas Mark 4 and bake for a further 30 minutes, or until the pastry is a light golden brown. Serve hot or cold, sprinkled with sugar.

lemon & passion fruit tart

serves 8
pastry

- 200 g/7 oz plain flour, plus extra for dusting
- pinch of salt
- 115 g/4 oz unsalted butter, chilled and diced
- 25 g/1 oz icing sugar, plus extra for dusting
- 1 egg yolk, blended with 2 tbsp ice-cold water

filling

- 4 passion fruit, plus extra to decorate
- juice and finely grated rind of 1 lemon
- 150 ml/5 fl oz double cream
- 4 tbsp crème fraîche
- 85 g/3 oz caster sugar
- 2 eggs
- 2 egg yolks

1 For the pastry, sift the flour and salt into a bowl. Rub in the butter with your fingertips until the mixture resembles fine breadcrumbs. Stir in the icing sugar and blended egg yolk and mix to a dough. Turn onto a floured work surface and knead until smooth. Wrap in clingfilm and chill in the refrigerator for 20 minutes.

2 Preheat the oven to 200°C/400°F/Gas Mark 6 and preheat a baking tray. Roll out the pastry on a lightly floured surface and use to line a 23-cm/9-inch loose-based fluted tart tin. Chill for 20 minutes.

3 Prick the pastry base all over, line with baking paper and fill with dried beans. Bake on the preheated baking tray for 10 minutes. Remove the paper and beans and return the pastry case to the oven for a further 5 minutes, until light golden. Reduce the oven temperature to 180°C/350°F/Gas Mark 4.

4 For the filling, halve the passion fruit and scoop out the seeds and pulp into a fine-mesh sieve set over a jug. Press with the back of a spoon until you have about 75 ml/2½ fl oz juice. Whisk together the passion fruit juice, lemon juice and rind, cream, crème fraîche, caster sugar, eggs and egg yolks until smooth. Pour into the pastry case. Bake for 30–35 minutes, until just set. Leave to cool completely. To serve, dust with icing sugar and decorate with passion fruit seeds and pulp.

sweet pumpkin pie

serves 6–8
filling
- 1.8 kg/4 lb pumpkin, quartered and deseeded
- 400 ml/14 fl oz condensed milk
- 2 eggs
- 1 tsp salt
- ½ tsp vanilla extract
- 1 tbsp demerara sugar

pastry
- 140 g/5 oz plain flour, plus extra for dusting
- ¼ tsp baking powder
- 1½ tsp ground cinnamon
- ¾ tsp ground nutmeg
- ¾ tsp ground cloves
- 50 g/1¾ oz caster sugar
- 55 g/2 oz unsalted butter, chilled and diced, plus extra for greasing
- 1 egg, beaten

topping
- 2 tbsp plain flour
- 4 tbsp demerara sugar
- 1 tbsp ground cinnamon
- 25 g/1 oz unsalted butter, chilled and diced
- 85 g/3 oz pecan nuts, chopped
- 70 g/2½ oz walnuts, chopped

1 Preheat the oven to 190°C/375°F/Gas Mark 5. Place the pumpkin quarters, skin-side up, in a roasting tin and cover with foil. Bake in the preheated oven for 1½ hours. Scoop out the flesh and purée in a food processor. Drain off any excess liquid, then cover and chill in the refrigerator.

2 Grease a 23-cm/9-inch pie dish. For the pastry, sift the flour and baking powder into a bowl. Stir in the spices and caster sugar. Rub in the butter with your fingertips until the mixture resembles breadcrumbs, then add the egg and mix to form a dough. Turn out onto a lightly floured work surface, roll out and use to line the prepared dish. Cover and chill in the refrigerator for 30 minutes.

3 Preheat the oven to 220°C/425°F/Gas Mark 7. For the filling, place the pumpkin purée in a large bowl, then stir in the condensed milk and eggs. Stir in the salt, vanilla extract and demerara sugar. Pour into the pastry case and bake in the preheated oven for 15 minutes.

4 Meanwhile, make the topping. Combine the flour, demerara sugar and cinnamon, then rub in the butter until crumbly and stir in the nuts. Remove the pie from the oven and reduce the oven temperature to 180°C/350°F/Gas Mark 4. Sprinkle over the topping, then bake for a further 35 minutes. Serve warm or cold.

pecan pie

serves 8
pastry
- 200 g/7 oz plain flour, plus extra for dusting
- 115 g/4 oz unsalted butter
- 2 tbsp caster sugar

filling
- 70 g/2½ oz unsalted butter
- 100 g/3½ oz light muscovado sugar
- 140 g/5 oz golden syrup
- 2 large eggs, beaten
- 1 tsp vanilla extract
- 115 g/4 oz pecan nuts

1 For the pastry, place the flour in a bowl and rub in the butter with your fingertips until it resembles fine breadcrumbs. Stir in the caster sugar and add enough cold water to mix to a firm dough. Wrap in clingfilm and chill in the refrigerator for 15 minutes, until firm enough to roll out.

2 Preheat the oven to 200°C/400°F/Gas Mark 6. Roll out the pastry on a lightly floured surface and use to line a 23-cm/9-inch loose-based tart tin. Prick the base with a fork. Chill for 15 minutes.

3 Place the tart tin on a baking tray, line with baking paper and fill with dried beans. Bake blind in the preheated oven for 10 minutes. Remove the paper and beans and bake for a further 5 minutes. Reduce the oven temperature to 180°C/350°F/Gas Mark 4.

4 For the filling, place the butter, muscovado sugar and golden syrup in a saucepan and heat gently until melted. Remove from the heat and quickly beat in the eggs and vanilla extract.

5 Roughly chop the pecans and stir into the mixture. Pour into the pastry case and bake for 35–40 minutes, until the filling is just set. Serve warm or cold.

summer fruit tartlets

makes 12

pastry

- 200 g/7 oz plain flour, plus extra for dusting
- 85 g/3 oz icing sugar
- 55 g/2 oz ground almonds
- 115 g/4 oz unsalted butter, diced and chilled
- 1 egg yolk
- 1 tbsp milk

filling

- 275 g/9¾ oz cream cheese
- icing sugar, to taste, plus extra for dusting
- 350 g/12 oz fresh mixed berries, such as blueberries, raspberries and strawberries

1 To make the pastry, sift the flour and icing sugar into a bowl, then stir in the ground almonds. Rub in the butter with your fingertips until the mixture resembles breadcrumbs. Add the egg yolk and milk and mix to form a dough. Turn out onto a lightly floured work surface and knead briefly. Wrap the dough in clingfilm and chill in the refrigerator for 30 minutes.

2 Preheat the oven to 200°C/400°F/Gas Mark 6.

3 Roll out the pastry and use it to line 12 deep tartlet or individual brioche tins. Prick the pastry bases with a fork. Press a piece of foil into each tartlet, covering the edges, and bake in the preheated oven for 10–15 minutes, or until light golden brown. Remove the foil and bake for a further 2–3 minutes. Transfer the pastry cases to a wire rack to cool.

4 To make the filling, mix the cream cheese and icing sugar together in a bowl. Put a spoonful of filling in each pastry case and arrange the berries on top. Dust with icing sugar and serve immediately.

apple strudel with cider sauce

serves 2–4

- 8 eating apples
- 1 tbsp lemon juice
- 115 g/4 oz sultanas
- 1 tsp ground cinnamon
- ½ tsp ground nutmeg
- 1 tbsp soft light brown sugar
- 6 sheets filo pastry, thawed, if frozen
- vegetable oil spray

sauce

- 1 tbsp cornflour
- 450 ml/16 fl oz dry cider

1 Preheat the oven to 190°C/375°F/Gas Mark 5. Line a baking tray with baking paper.

2 Peel and core the apples and chop them into 1-cm/½-inch dice. Toss the apples in a bowl with the lemon juice, sultanas, cinnamon, nutmeg and brown sugar.

3 Lay out a sheet of filo pastry, spray with vegetable oil and lay a second sheet on top. Repeat with a third sheet. Spread over half the apple mixture and roll up lengthways, tucking in the ends to enclose the filling. Repeat to make a second strudel. Slide onto the prepared baking tray, spray with oil and bake in the preheated oven for 15–20 minutes.

4 To make the sauce, blend the cornflour in a saucepan with a little cider until smooth. Add the remaining cider and heat gently, stirring, until the mixture boils and thickens. Serve the strudel warm or cold accompanied by the cider sauce.

strawberry cream cobbler

serves 4
- 800 g/1 lb 12 oz strawberries, hulled and halved
- 50 g/1¾ oz caster sugar
- clotted cream, to serve

cobbler topping
- 200 g/7 oz self-raising flour, plus extra for dusting
- pinch of salt
- 40 g/1½ oz unsalted butter
- 2 tbsp caster sugar
- 1 egg, beaten
- 25 g/1 oz sultanas
- 25 g/1 oz currants
- about 5 tbsp milk, plus extra for glazing

1 Preheat the oven to 200°C/400°F/Gas Mark 6.

2 Arrange the strawberries evenly in the bottom of an ovenproof dish, then sprinkle over the sugar and cook in the preheated oven for 5–10 minutes, until heated through.

3 Meanwhile, to make the cobbler topping, sift the flour and salt into a large mixing bowl. Rub in the butter with your fingertips until the mixture resembles fine breadcrumbs, then stir in the sugar. Add the egg, sultanas and currants, and mix lightly until incorporated. Stir in enough of the milk to make a smooth dough.

4 Transfer to a lightly floured work surface and knead lightly, then roll out to a thickness of about 1 cm/½ inch. Cut out rounds using a 5-cm/2-inch biscuit cutter. Arrange the dough rounds over the strawberries, then brush the tops with a little milk.

5 Bake in the preheated oven for 25–30 minutes, or until the cobbler topping has risen and is lightly golden. Serve hot with clotted cream.

apple & blackberry crumble

serves 4
- 900 g/2 lb cooking apples
- 300 g/10½ oz blackberries, fresh or frozen
- 55 g/2 oz light muscovado sugar
- 1 tsp ground cinnamon

crumble topping
- 85 g/3 oz white self-raising flour
- 85 g/3 oz wholemeal plain flour
- 115 g/4 oz unsalted butter
- 55 g/2 oz demerara sugar

1 Preheat the oven to 190°C/375°F/Gas Mark 5.

2 Peel and core the apples and cut into chunks. Place in a bowl with the blackberries, muscovado sugar and cinnamon and mix together, then transfer to an ovenproof baking dish.

3 To make the crumble topping, sift the white flour into a bowl and stir in the wholemeal flour. Add the butter and rub in with your fingers until the mixture resembles fine breadcrumbs. Stir in the demerara sugar.

4 Spread the crumble over the apple mixture and bake in the preheated oven for 40–45 minutes, or until the apples are soft and the crumble topping is golden brown and crisp.

Mmmm...
bread &
savouries

irish soda bread

makes 1 loaf

- butter, for greasing
- 450 g/1 lb plain flour, plus extra for dusting
- 1 tsp salt
- 1 tsp bicarbonate of soda
- 400 ml/14 fl oz buttermilk

1 Preheat the oven to 220°C/425°F/Gas Mark 7. Lightly grease a baking tray.

2 Sift the flour, salt and bicarbonate of soda into a mixing bowl. Make a well in the centre of the dry ingredients and pour in most of the buttermilk.

3 Mix well together using your hands. The dough should be very soft but not too wet. If necessary, add the remaining buttermilk.

4 Turn out the dough onto a lightly floured work surface and knead it lightly. Shape into a 20-cm/8-inch round.

5 Place on the prepared baking tray, cut a cross in the top and bake in the preheated oven for 25–30 minutes, until golden brown and it sounds hollow when tapped on the base.

crusty white bread

makes 1 loaf
- 1 egg
- 1 egg yolk
- 500 g/1 lb 2 oz white strong flour, plus extra for dusting
- 1½ tsp salt
- 2 tsp sugar
- 1 tsp easy-blend dried yeast
- 25 g/1 oz butter, diced
- sunflower oil, for oiling

1 Place the egg and egg yolk in a jug and beat lightly to mix. Add enough lukewarm water to make up to 300 ml/10 fl oz. Stir well.

2 Place the flour, salt, sugar and yeast in a large bowl. Add the butter and rub it in with your fingertips until the mixture resembles breadcrumbs. Make a well in the centre, add the egg mixture and work to a smooth dough.

3 Turn out onto a lightly floured work surface and knead well for about 10 minutes, until smooth. Brush a bowl with oil. Shape the dough into a ball, place it in the bowl and cover with a damp tea towel. Leave to rise in a warm place for 1 hour, until the dough has doubled in volume.

4 Oil a 900-g/2-lb loaf tin. Turn the dough out onto a lightly floured work surface and knead for 1 minute, until smooth. Shape the dough the length of the tin and 3 times the width. Fold the dough into 3 lengthways and place it in the tin with the join underneath. Cover and leave in a warm place for 30 minutes, until it has risen above the rim of the tin.

5 Preheat the oven to 220°C/425°F/Gas Mark 7. Bake in the preheated oven for 30 minutes, or until firm and it sounds hollow when tapped on the base. Transfer to a wire rack to cool.

wholemeal harvest bread

makes 1 loaf

- 225 g/8 oz wholemeal strong flour, plus extra for dusting
- 1 tbsp skimmed milk powder
- 1 tsp salt
- 2 tbsp soft light brown sugar
- 1 tsp easy-blend dried yeast
- 1½ tbsp sunflower oil, plus extra for oiling
- 175 ml/6 fl oz lukewarm water

1 Place the flour, milk powder, salt, sugar and yeast in a large bowl. Pour in the oil and add the water, then mix well to make a smooth dough.

2 Turn out onto a lightly floured work surface and knead well for about 10 minutes, until smooth. Brush a bowl with oil. Shape the dough into a ball, place it in the bowl and cover with a damp tea towel. Leave to rise in a warm place for 1 hour, until the dough has doubled in volume.

3 Oil a 900-g/2-lb loaf tin. Turn the dough out onto a lightly floured work surface and knead for 1 minute, until smooth. Shape the dough the length of the tin and 3 times the width. Fold the dough into 3 lengthways and place it in the tin with the join underneath. Cover and leave in a warm place for 30 minutes, until it has risen above the rim of the tin.

4 Preheat the oven to 220°C/425°F/Gas Mark 7. Place in the preheated oven and bake for 30 minutes, or until golden brown and it sounds hollow when tapped on the base. Transfer to a wire rack to cool.

blue cheese, fig & walnut bread

makes 1 loaf

- 85 g/3 oz dried figs, roughly chopped
- 4 tbsp Marsala
- butter, for greasing
- 200 g/7 oz plain flour
- 1 tbsp baking powder
- 3 eggs
- 200 g/7 oz crème fraîche
- 175 g/6 oz blue cheese, such as Roquefort or Gorgonzola, crumbled
- 75 g/2¾ oz walnuts, roughly chopped
- salt and pepper

1 Put the figs in a small bowl, pour over the Marsala and leave to soak for 30 minutes.

2 Preheat the oven to 180°C/350°F/Gas Mark 4. Lightly grease a 450-g/1-lb loaf tin and line with baking paper.

3 Sift the flour and baking powder into a large bowl. In a separate bowl, beat the eggs and crème fraîche together until smooth. Stir the egg mixture into the flour mixture until well combined. Season to taste with salt and a good grinding of pepper.

4 Add 150 g/5½ oz of the blue cheese, the figs and the Marsala, then stir in half the walnuts. Turn the mixture into the prepared tin, scatter over the remaining cheese and walnuts and bake in the preheated oven for 40 minutes, or until the loaf is golden brown.

5 Cover the tin loosely with foil and return to the oven for a further 15 minutes, or until a skewer inserted into the centre of the loaf comes out clean. Leave to cool slightly in the tin, then turn out onto a wire rack to cool completely.

muesli bread

makes 1 loaf

- 300 g/10½ oz white strong flour, plus extra for dusting
- 85 g/3 oz wholemeal strong flour
- 1½ tsp salt
- 150 g/5½ oz unsweetened muesli
- 3 tbsp skimmed milk powder
- 1½ tsp easy-blend dried yeast
- 225 ml/8 fl oz lukewarm water
- 2 tbsp vegetable oil, plus extra for brushing
- 1 tbsp honey
- 70 g/2½ oz ready-to-eat dried apricots, chopped

1 Sift the flours and salt together into a bowl, adding any bran left in the sieve. Stir in the muesli, milk powder and yeast. Make a well in the centre and pour in the lukewarm water, oil and honey. Stir well with a wooden spoon until the dough begins to come together, then mix with your hands to form a dough.

2 Turn out onto a lightly floured work surface and knead well for 5 minutes. Add the apricots and knead for a further 5 minutes, until the dough is smooth and elastic.

3 Brush a bowl with oil. Shape the dough into a ball, place it in the bowl and cover with clingfilm. Leave to rise in a warm place for 1 hour, until the dough has doubled in volume.

4 Brush a baking tray with oil. Turn out the dough onto a lightly floured work surface and knock back with your fist. Shape the dough into a round and place on the prepared baking tray. Cut a cross in the top of the loaf. Cover the baking tray with a damp tea towel and leave to rise in a warm place for 30–40 minutes.

5 Preheat the oven to 200°C/400°F/Gas Mark 6. Bake the loaf for 30–35 minutes, until golden brown and it sounds hollow when tapped on the base. Transfer to a wire rack to cool.

olive & sun-dried tomato bread

makes 2 loaves

- 400 g/14 oz plain flour, plus extra for dusting
- 1 tsp salt
- 1 sachet (about 7 g/¼ oz) easy-blend dried yeast
- 1 tsp brown sugar
- 1 tbsp chopped fresh thyme
- 200 ml/7 fl oz lukewarm water
- 4 tbsp olive oil, plus extra for brushing
- 55 g/2 oz black olives, stoned and sliced
- 55 g/2 oz green olives, stoned and sliced
- 100 g/3½ oz sun-dried tomatoes in oil, drained and sliced
- 1 egg yolk, beaten

1 Sift the flour and salt together into a bowl and stir in the yeast, sugar and thyme. Make a well in the centre and pour in the lukewarm water and oil. Stir well with a wooden spoon until the mixture begins to come together, then mix with your hands to form a dough.

2 Turn out onto a lightly floured work surface and add the olives and sun-dried tomatoes, then knead for a further 5 minutes, until the dough is smooth and elastic.

3 Brush a bowl with oil. Shape the dough into a ball, place it in the bowl and cover with clingfilm. Leave to rise in a warm place for 1–1½ hours, until the dough has doubled in volume.

4 Dust a baking tray with flour. Turn out the dough onto a lightly floured work surface and knock back with your fist. Cut it in half and shape each half into a round. Put them on the prepared baking tray and cover with a damp tea towel. Leave to rise in a warm place for 45 minutes.

5 Preheat the oven to 200°C/400°F/Gas Mark 6. Make 3 shallow diagonal slashes on the top of each loaf and brush with the egg yolk. Bake for 40 minutes, until golden brown and the loaves sound hollow when tapped on the bases. Transfer to a wire rack to cool.

tomato & rosemary focaccia

makes 1 loaf

- 500 g/1 lb 2 oz white strong flour, plus extra for dusting
- 1½ tsp salt
- 1½ tsp easy-blend dried yeast
- 2 tbsp chopped fresh rosemary, plus extra sprigs to garnish
- 6 tbsp extra virgin olive oil, plus extra for brushing
- 300 ml/10 fl oz lukewarm water
- 6 oven-dried or sun-blush tomato halves, sliced
- 1 tsp coarse sea salt

1 Sift the flour and salt together into a bowl and stir in the yeast and rosemary. Make a well in the centre, pour in 4 tablespoons of the oil and mix quickly with a wooden spoon. Gradually stir in the lukewarm water but do not over-mix. Turn out onto a lightly floured work surface and knead for 2 minutes. The dough will be quite wet; do not add more flour.

2 Brush a bowl with oil. Shape the dough into a ball, put it in the bowl and cover with clingfilm. Leave to rise in a warm place for 2 hours, until the dough has doubled in volume.

3 Brush a baking tray with oil. Turn out the dough onto a lightly floured work surface and knock back with your fist, then knead for 1 minute. Put the dough on the prepared baking tray and press out into an even layer. Cover the baking tray with a damp tea towel. Leave to rise in a warm place for 1 hour.

4 Preheat the oven to 240°C/475°F/Gas Mark 9. Whisk the remaining oil with a little water in a bowl. Dip your fingers into the oil mixture and press them into the dough to make dimples all over. Sprinkle with the tomatoes, salt and rosemary sprigs. Reduce the oven temperature to 220°C/425°F/Gas Mark 7 and bake the focaccia for 20 minutes, until golden brown. Transfer to a wire rack to cool slightly before serving.

corn bread

makes 1 loaf
- vegetable oil, for brushing
- 175 g/6 oz plain flour
- 1 tsp salt
- 4 tsp baking powder
- 1 tsp caster sugar
- 280 g/10 oz polenta
- 115 g/4 oz butter, softened
- 4 eggs
- 225 ml/8 fl oz milk
- 3 tbsp double cream

1 Preheat the oven to 200°C/400°F/Gas Mark 6. Brush a 20-cm/8-inch square cake tin with oil.

2 Sift the flour, salt and baking powder together into a bowl. Add the sugar and polenta and stir to mix. Add the butter and cut it into the dry ingredients with a knife, then rub in with your fingertips until the mixture resembles breadcrumbs.

3 Lightly beat the eggs in a bowl with the milk and cream, then stir into the polenta mixture until thoroughly combined.

4 Spoon the mixture into the prepared tin and smooth the surface. Bake in the preheated oven for 30–35 minutes, until a skewer inserted into the centre of the loaf comes out clean. Remove the tin from the oven and leave to cool for 5–10 minutes, then cut into squares and serve warm.

wholemeal cheddar scones

makes 12

- sunflower oil, for brushing
- 225 g/8 oz wholemeal self-raising flour, plus extra for dusting
- 1 tsp English mustard powder
- 1 tsp salt
- 40 g/1½ oz butter, chilled and finely diced
- 115 g/4 oz mature Cheddar cheese, grated
- 2 tbsp snipped fresh chives
- about 150 ml/5 fl oz milk, plus extra for glazing

1 Preheat the oven to 220°C/425°F/Gas Mark 7. Very lightly brush a baking tray with oil.

2 Put the flour, mustard powder and salt into a food processor and process until blended. Add the butter and quickly process until crumbs form, then stir in the cheese and chives and process again. Slowly add just enough milk to make a soft, light dough, taking care not to over-process the dough.

3 Turn out the dough onto a lightly floured work surface and pat out with a lightly floured rolling pin until it is about 2 cm/¾ inch thick. Handle the dough as little as possible. Use a 5-cm/2-inch round biscuit cutter to stamp out 12 scones, re-rolling the trimmings as necessary.

4 Place the scones on the prepared baking tray and brush the tops with milk. Bake in the preheated oven for 10 minutes, or until risen and golden brown on top. Transfer to a wire rack to cool.

chunky apple & cheese muffins

makes 12

- oil or melted butter, for greasing (if using)
- 250 g/9 oz plain flour
- 1 tbsp baking powder
- ½ tsp salt
- 4 tbsp sunflower oil
- 150 g/5½ oz low-fat natural yogurt
- 2 eggs, beaten
- 125 ml/4 fl oz milk
- 140 g/5 oz extra-mature Cheddar cheese, coarsely grated
- 2 dessert apples, cored and cut into 5-mm/¼-inch dice
- 55 g/2 oz sultanas

1 Preheat the oven to 190°C/375°F/Gas Mark 5. Grease a 12-cup muffin tin or line with 12 paper muffin cases.

2 Sift the flour, baking powder and salt into a large bowl and make a well in the centre. Add the oil, yogurt, eggs and milk, then mix well to combine evenly.

3 Reserve about 2 tablespoons of the cheese and add the rest to the bowl with the apples and sultanas, stirring lightly to mix.

4 Spoon the mixture into the prepared muffin tin and sprinkle with the reserved cheese. Bake in the preheated oven for 20–25 minutes, or until well risen and golden brown.

5 Leave the muffins in the tin for 5 minutes, then serve warm.

courgette & sesame seed muffins

makes 12

- oil or melted butter, for greasing (if using)
- 300 g/10½ oz small firm courgettes
- 280 g/10 oz plain flour
- 1 tbsp baking powder
- ⅛ tsp salt
- 6 tsp sesame seeds
- ½ tsp dried mixed herbs
- 2 eggs
- 250 ml/9 fl oz buttermilk
- 6 tbsp sunflower oil or 85 g/ 3 oz butter, melted and cooled
- pepper

1 Preheat the oven to 200°C/400°F/Gas Mark 6. Grease a 12-cup tin or line with 12 paper muffin cases. Grate the courgettes, squeezing out any excess moisture.

2 Sift together the flour, baking powder, salt and pepper to taste into a large bowl. Stir in 4 teaspoons of the sesame seeds and the mixed herbs.

3 Lightly beat the eggs in a large jug or bowl, then beat in the buttermilk and oil. Make a well in the centre of the dry ingredients, pour in the beaten liquid ingredients and add the courgettes. Stir gently until just combined; do not over-mix.

4 Spoon the mixture into the prepared muffin tin. Scatter the remaining sesame seeds over the tops of the muffins. Bake in the preheated oven for about 20 minutes, until well risen, golden brown and firm to the touch.

5 Leave the muffins in the tin for 5 minutes, then serve warm.

italian pesto muffins

makes 12

- oil or melted butter, for greasing (if using)
- 280 g/10 oz plain flour
- 1 tbsp baking powder
- ⅛ tsp salt
- 50 g/1¾ oz pine kernels
- 2 eggs
- 150 ml/5 fl oz buttermilk
- 6 tbsp sunflower oil or 85 g/ 3 oz butter, melted and cooled
- 6 tbsp pesto
- 10 g/¼ oz Parmesan cheese, grated
- pepper

1 Preheat the oven to 200°C/400°F/Gas Mark 6. Grease a 12-cup muffin tin or line with 12 paper muffin cases.

2 Sift together the flour, baking powder, salt and pepper to taste into a large bowl. Stir in the pine kernels.

3 Lightly beat the eggs in a large jug or bowl, then beat in the buttermilk, oil and pesto. Make a well in the centre of the dry ingredients and pour in the beaten liquid ingredients. Stir gently until just combined; do not over-mix.

4 Spoon the mixture into the prepared muffin tin. Scatter the Parmesan cheese over the tops of the muffins. Bake in the preheated oven for about 20 minutes, until well risen, golden brown and firm to the touch.

5 Leave the muffins in the tin for 5 minutes, then serve warm.

savoury oat crackers

makes 12-14

- 100 g/3½ oz unsalted butter, plus extra for greasing
- 90 g/3¼ oz porridge oats
- 25 g/1 oz wholemeal plain flour
- ½ tsp coarse sea salt
- 1 tsp dried thyme
- 40 g/1½ oz walnuts, finely chopped
- 1 egg, beaten
- 40 g/1½ oz sesame seeds

1 Preheat the oven to 180°C/350°F/Gas Mark 4. Lightly grease 2 baking trays.

2 Rub the butter into the oats and flour with your fingertips. Stir in the salt, thyme and walnuts, then add the egg and mix to a soft dough.

3 Spread out the sesame seeds on a large shallow plate or tray. Break off walnut-sized pieces of dough and roll into balls, then roll in the sesame seeds to coat lightly and evenly.

4 Place the balls of dough on the prepared baking trays, spaced well apart, and roll the rolling pin over them to flatten as much as possible. Bake in the preheated oven for 12–15 minutes, or until firm and pale golden.

5 Leave to cool on the baking trays for 3–4 minutes, then transfer to a wire rack to finish cooling.

cheese sablés

makes about 35
- 150 g/5½ oz plain flour, plus extra for dusting
- 150 g/5½ oz mature Cheddar cheese, grated
- 150 g/5½ oz butter, diced, plus extra for greasing
- 1 egg yolk
- 3 tbsp sesame seeds

1 Mix the flour and cheese together in a bowl. Add the butter to the cheese and flour mixture and rub in with your fingertips until combined.

2 Stir in the egg yolk and mix to form a dough. Wrap the dough in clingfilm and leave to chill in the refrigerator for about 30 minutes.

3 Preheat the oven to 200°C/400°F/Gas Mark 6. Lightly grease several baking trays.

4 On a lightly floured work surface, roll out the dough thinly. Stamp out 6-cm/2½-inch rounds with a biscuit cutter, re-rolling the trimmings to make about 35 rounds.

5 Place the rounds on the prepared baking trays and sprinkle the sesame seeds over the top of them.

6 Bake in the preheated oven for 10 minutes, until the sablés are light golden in colour. Carefully transfer the cheese sablés to a wire rack and leave to cool slightly before serving.

cheese straws

makes about 24

- 115 g/4 oz plain flour, plus extra for dusting
- pinch of salt
- 1 tsp curry powder
- 55 g/2 oz butter, plus extra for greasing
- 55 g/2 oz grated Cheddar cheese
- 1 egg, beaten
- 1 tbsp each poppy and cumin seeds

1 Sift the flour, salt and curry powder into a bowl. Add the butter and rub in with your fingertips until the mixture resembles breadcrumbs. Add the cheese and half the egg and mix to form a dough. Wrap in clingfilm and chill in the refrigerator for 30 minutes.

2 Preheat the oven to 200°C/400°F/Gas Mark 6. Grease 2 baking trays.

3 On a floured work surface, roll out the dough to 5 mm/¼ inch thick. Cut into 7.5 x 1-cm/3 x ½-inch strips. Pinch the strips lightly along the sides and place on the prepared baking trays.

4 Brush with the remaining egg and sprinkle half the strips with the poppy seeds and half with the cumin seeds. Bake in the preheated oven for 10–15 minutes, or until golden. Transfer to wire racks to cool.

quiche lorraine

serves 6–8
pastry

- 200 g/7 oz plain flour, plus extra for dusting
- 100 g/3½ oz butter
- 1–2 tbsp cold water

filling

- 15 g/½ oz butter
- 1 small onion, finely chopped
- 4 lean streaky bacon rashers, diced
- 55 g/2 oz Gruyère cheese or Cheddar cheese, grated
- 2 eggs, beaten
- 300 ml/10 fl oz single cream
- pepper

1 For the pastry, sift the flour into a bowl and rub in the butter with your fingertips until the mixture resembles fine breadcrumbs. Stir in just enough of the water to make a firm dough.

2 Roll out the dough on a lightly floured work surface, then use to line a 23-cm/9-inch loose-based tart tin. Trim the edges and prick the base all over with a fork. Chill in the refrigerator for at least 10 minutes.

3 Preheat the oven to 200°C/400°F/Gas Mark 6 and preheat a baking tray. Line the pastry case with baking paper and fill with dried beans. Place on the baking tray and bake in the preheated oven for 10 minutes. Remove the paper and beans and bake for a further 10 minutes.

4 For the filling, melt the butter in a frying pan and cook the onion and bacon over a medium heat for about 5 minutes. Spread evenly over the hot pastry case and sprinkle with half the cheese. Beat together the eggs and cream and season to taste with pepper. Pour into the pastry case and sprinkle with the remaining cheese.

5 Reduce the oven temperature to 190°C/375°F/Gas Mark 5. Place the quiche in the oven and bake for 25–30 minutes, or until golden brown and just set. Leave to cool for 10 minutes before turning out.

leek & onion tartlets

makes 6
- butter, for greasing
- 225 g/8 oz ready-made shortcrust pastry
- plain flour, for dusting

filling
- 25 g/1 oz unsalted butter
- 1 onion, thinly sliced
- 450 g/1 lb leeks, thinly sliced
- 2 tsp chopped fresh thyme
- 55 g/2 oz Gruyère cheese, grated
- 3 eggs
- 300 ml/10 fl oz double cream
- salt and pepper

1 Lightly grease 6 x 10-cm/4-inch tartlet tins. Roll out the pastry on a lightly floured work surface and stamp out 6 rounds with a 13-cm/5-inch biscuit cutter. Use to line the prepared tins, trim the edges and prick the bases all over with a fork. Chill in the refrigerator for 30 minutes.

2 Preheat the oven to 190°C/ 375°F/Gas Mark 5. Line the pastry cases with foil and fill with dried beans, then place on a baking tray and bake in the preheated oven for 8 minutes. Remove the foil and beans and bake for a further 2 minutes. Transfer to a wire rack to cool. Reduce the oven temperature to 180°C/350°F/Gas Mark 4.

3 Meanwhile, make the filling. Melt the butter in a large heavy-based frying pan. Add the onion and cook, stirring constantly, for 5 minutes, or until softened. Add the leeks and thyme and cook, stirring, for 10 minutes, or until softened. Divide the mixture among the pastry cases. Sprinkle with the cheese.

4 Beat together the eggs and cream and season to taste with salt and pepper. Pour into the pastry cases and place on a baking tray. Bake for 15 minutes, or until golden brown and just set. Leave to cool slightly before turning out.

vegetable jalousie

serves 4

- 25 g/1 oz butter
- 1 leek, shredded
- 2 garlic cloves, crushed
- 50 g/1¾ oz mushrooms, sliced
- 1 red pepper, deseeded and sliced
- 1 yellow pepper, deseeded and sliced
- 75 g/2¾ oz small asparagus spears
- 2 tbsp plain flour, plus extra for dusting
- 6 tbsp vegetable stock
- 6 tbsp milk
- 4 tbsp dry white wine
- 1 tbsp chopped fresh oregano
- 450 g/1 lb ready-made puff pastry
- 1 egg, beaten
- salt and pepper

1 Preheat the oven to 200°C/400°F/Gas Mark 6. Dampen a sheet of baking paper with water and use to line a baking tray.

2 For the filling, melt the butter in a saucepan. Add the leek and garlic and sauté for 2 minutes. Stir in the remaining vegetables and cook for 3–4 minutes.

3 Add the flour and cook for 1 minute. Remove from the heat and stir in the stock, milk and wine. Return to the heat and bring to the boil, stirring, until thickened. Stir in the oregano and season to taste with salt and pepper.

4 Roll out half the pastry on a lightly floured work surface to form a rectangle measuring 38 x 15 cm/ 15 x 6 inches. Roll out the other half into a slightly larger rectangle. Place the smaller rectangle on the prepared baking tray.

5 Spoon the filling on top of the smaller rectangle, leaving a 1-cm/½-inch margin all around. Cut parallel slits across the larger rectangle to within 2.5 cm/1 inch of each edge. Brush around the edges of the smaller rectangle with a little of the beaten egg and place the larger rectangle on top, sealing the edges well. Brush with the remaining beaten egg and bake in the preheated oven for 30–35 minutes, until risen and golden.

mushroom & spinach parcels

makes 4

- 25 g/1 oz butter
- 1 red onion, halved and sliced
- 2 garlic cloves, crushed
- 225 g/8 oz open-cap mushrooms, sliced
- 175 g/6 oz baby spinach
- pinch of nutmeg
- 4 tbsp double cream
- 225 g/8 oz ready-made puff pastry
- plain flour, for dusting
- 1 egg, beaten
- 2 tsp poppy seeds
- salt and pepper

1 Preheat the oven to 200°C/400°F/Gas Mark 6. Dampen a baking tray with water.

2 Melt the butter in a frying pan. Add the onion and garlic and sauté for 3–4 minutes, until the onion has softened.

3 Add the mushrooms, spinach and nutmeg and cook for a further 2–3 minutes. Stir in the cream, mixing well. Season to taste with salt and pepper and remove the frying pan from the heat.

4 Roll the pastry out on a lightly floured work surface and cut into 4 x 15-cm/6-inch rounds. Spoon a quarter of the filling onto half of each round and fold the pastry over to encase the filling. Press down to seal the edges of the pastry and brush with the beaten egg. Sprinkle with the poppy seeds.

5 Place the parcels onto the prepared baking tray and cook in the preheated oven for 20 minutes, until risen and golden brown.

6 Transfer the parcels to serving plates and serve immediately.

hot cheese pastries

makes 32

- 200 g/7 oz feta cheese
- 115 g/4 oz cottage cheese
- 3 tbsp chopped fresh flat-leaf parsley
- 2 eggs, beaten
- 8 sheets filo pastry
- 100 ml/3½ fl oz olive oil
- pepper

1 Preheat the oven to 190°C/375°F/Gas Mark 5. Oil 2 baking trays.

2 Crumble the feta cheese into a bowl. Add the cottage cheese, parsley and eggs and beat together with a fork until well blended. Season to taste with pepper.

3 Cut the filo pastry, down the longest length, into 4 strips, each about 7 cm/2¾ inches wide. Take a strip and cover the remaining strips with a damp tea towel. Brush the strip with a little of the oil and put a heaped teaspoon of the cheese mixture on the bottom left-hand corner. Fold over the corner with the filling so that it meets the long side edge and forms a triangle. Continue folding the filling up and over from side to side to form a neat triangle. Place the triangle on a prepared baking tray and brush with oil. Continue until all the pastry strips and the filling have been used.

4 Bake the pastries in the preheated oven for about 15 minutes, until golden brown. Serve hot.

Index